Mark My Words

A study of teachers as correctors of children's writing

TONY DUNSBEE
with
Terry Ford

Ward Lock Educational
in association with
NATE

ISBN 0 7062 3932 6

First published 1980

Set in 11 on 12 point Baskerville by Jubal Multiwrite Ltd, London SE13
Reproduced from copy supplied
printed and bound in Great Britain
by Billing and Sons Limited
Guildford, London, Oxford, Worcester

Contents

List of test scripts and figures

Acknowledgments

Tony Dunsbee is a senior member of the English department, Myton School, Warwick.

Terry Ford was warden of the Mid-Warwickshire Teachers' Centre, Leamington Spa, when the book was written.

The research described in this study was undertaken jointly. The text was written by Tony Dunsbee.

We gratefully acknowledge the cooperation and assistance of the head teachers, staff and pupils of the following schools where our original investigations and enquiries were conducted:

Myton School, Warwick
Park Hill Middle School, Kenilworth
Baddesley Clinton Primary School, near Knowle, West Midlands

In respect of his contribution to our initial understanding of some of the problems raised by our researches, we should here like to record our gratitude to the late Harry Raistrick, of the Warwickshire County Inspectorate.

Our thanks go to NATE and the members of Publications Committee; to Pat D'Arcy for her initial encouragement, and to Mike Torbe for helping us through to publication.

And on a final, more personal note, we not only wish to thank Jenny Blake for her secretarial help when our study went to the first stage of local dissemination, but also our respective wives and families for their forbearance and tolerance during the past three years.

Preface

When Tony Dunsbee sent me an earlier draft of *Mark My Words,* it began with this quote.

> Interest and participation in research are increasingly open to the teacher — they are part of the contemporary educational climate; but discrimination and judgment of the processes in research terms are not within his normal province, nor are intuition, and long experience of his own expertise of teaching, any substitutes.
>
> Roland Harris (1967)

He commented on the difficulties for teachers of actually involving themselves in research, and suggested that *Mark My Words* itself was an example of what a teacher could do, because a teacher had done it.

There is a complicated set of responses in teachers towards research, that mirrors the ambiguities in Harris's comment (what he actually feels about teachers is not as clear as it might be). We can notice, with something between resentment and envy, the way in which the life and work of the researcher is remote from the hurly-burly of teacher and children in classrooms. We can react strongly against the lordly way in which pronouncements can be made.

> It was suggested that there is now adequate research for improving spelling; the problem is that this research is not being applied. The task therefore would seem to be to make teachers aware of the findings of research studies.
>
> *Spelling; task and learner* Wade & Weddell: *Educational Review Occasional Publications* 5. 1974

We can — rightly! — be incensed at the patronising way researchers can survey their raw material as though teachers and children have no independent life of their own; or as if theirs is a lesser, uncivilized form of life.

We have watched the school island through a telescope from the ship anchored in the bay long enough. Now that one of the explorers has returned with the news that the natives are friendly (even if slightly misguided), let us have a few more landing parties. There are many more native villages to explore.

Review of *Classrooms Observed* by
Roland Hoste, *Educational Research*, 16.2

On the other hand, there is a lurking respect for institutions like universities or research bodies. The people who work in such institutions must — mustn't they? — be more intelligent. Even when part of our mind tells us that's not so, the other half insists that it *is* so. And that means — the last temptation, and the greatest treason — that if teachers do try to write about their teaching, they tend to try and do it in the ways they feel are respectable, in the forms and styles of 'research'.

Well, *Mark My Words* isn't research. It is an investigation of a small area of everyday practice, which illuminates, in an unexpected way, one aspect of teaching and learning. Why isn't it research? Because it isn't 'rigorous', nothing was held constant as a control, no attempt was made to screen out variables, no statistical patterns are derived from the data, and the conclusions are subjective impressions. And yet — what should action research look like? It should, I suppose, be something that the readers know in their guts is right, irrespective of whether they want to agree with it or not; it should be able to be repeated in outline by others to test the kinds of practical conclusions drawn; but, above all, it should derive directly from experience and immediately cycle back to affect that experience.

It's here, then, that most educational research has failed: the data is abstracted from the field of action and the research then makes pronouncements *about the data* and not about what is really at issue, the effective behaviour of people interacting in particular contexts. When the research findings reach the original creators of the data, namely the teachers and pupils themselves, they have become alienated from it by the process by which it has come into being and probably also by the form and language in which it is expressed. So the difficulty for teachers in being involved in a good deal of research is also a declaration that that research is not the kind that is relevant, because the assumptions it makes are not those that teachers, on the whole, particularly share.

There are kinds of research that are distinguished by their refusal to take an Olympian stance of detachment, which insist on the humanity of participants, and assert their individuality instead of reducing them to numbers. Elizabeth Richardson's Nailsea research, documented especially in *The Teacher, The School and The Task of Management* (Heinemann) is, to my mind, an example of research that tries to synthesize rather than categorize.

One other simple problem makes it hard for teachers to be researchers: not 'discriminations and judgment of the processes in research terms', but *time* — the time it takes to collect the data, and to write about it. And being prepared and willing to get involved in such an enterprise at all is an investment. After all, why bother? What's in it for the teacher? An answer to that question — or a part-answer — will be found in this book. *Mark My Words* demonstrates that asking some simple questions and setting out to find ways of answering them, has powerful pay-offs. And isn't that a description of what research ought to be?

Mike Torbe

1 Gaining a perspective

Introduction

The theme of this book is the fruitful correction and criticism of children's writing in all subjects of the curriculum. An activity perhaps rightly regarded as one of the last bastions of teacher-autonomy, it has hardly been researched to date — possibly (and self-evidently) because this might threaten certain freedoms which teachers have traditionally enjoyed, but also because 'marking' is a task frequently carried out in private, away from the classroom. This book therefore offers its readers insights into possibly the most mundane aspect of any class-room teacher's daily and weekly routine, in the belief that taking a fresh look at the commonplace will demonstrate that the only valid research for teachers is that which holds out the promise of increasing our effectiveness. How a more effective appraisal of children's writing abilities might be made has rarely been discussed on teacher-training courses or by school staffs — using the term 'appraisal' here as Joan Tough (1976) has used it, to denote 'keeping the child's growing skill in using language in view, as a guide to the action that the teacher might take'. This concept seems helpful and there is no doubt that the current trend towards accountability should make us reconsider carefully what we are doing when we 'mark' class-work or homework. If we don't, how can we justify the respect we afford the activity to either our pupils or the wider com-munity of parents, governors and interested adults?

Regrettably, 'marking' has always been a thorn in the educa-tionist's flesh. It's there, but we wish it would go away, because it has nothing to do with 'real teaching' as we would prefer to envisage it. Nevertheless, occasional lip-service has been paid to the opinion of some teachers that 'marking', a necessary yet time-consuming evil, is much in need of reform and in every major educational report published this century, there has always been at least a passing reference to the problem. In spite of this fitful interest, however, solutions seem no nearer to hand.

1

In recent years, the influential Schools Council Working Paper No 3 (1965) suggested that one direction to be taken was 'to set out the problems of assessment and correction, and supply some of the answers'. But this was overlooked in the attempt to comply with the simultaneous suggestion that the various stages in the development of writing abilities should be mapped out. Ten years later, the Bullock Report (1975) reiterated a similar concern, but with less sense of either commitment or urgency:

> ... there has been a welcome increase in opportunities for teachers to discuss the assessment of children's written work. This has ranged from the experience of inter-school assessment and moderation in 16+ examinations to the informal study of primary school children's writing in teachers' centres. We should like to see such opportunities taken up more widely, for we have no doubt that the understanding that grows from them can have a considerable influence on the development of children's writing.

At first sight, the ignoring of these two appeals in the last fourteen years may not seem to be very strong grounds for complaint. After all, reports are always full of perfectly sound ideas that are overlooked for one reason or another. However, a formal investigation of marking practices in schools was also mooted by the then Board of Education in 1937, so that we are concerned with a period of neglect extending for at least forty years, not merely fourteen.

An assumption now prevails to the effect that genuinely enlightened teachers don't 'mark' extended pieces of written work. This certainly emerges from a study of books about the teaching of English, in which the desultory 'marking' most serving teachers would recognize as being close to reality is roundly condemned. Yet, setting aside for the moment the pros and cons of the various approaches to 'marking' that teachers can and do employ, it is extraordinary that such scant attention should have been given, over such a long period of time, to what is (by virtue of the hours it habitually consumes) a major teacher-activity. Despite new teaching methods, 'marking' continues to represent virtually the sole means of written mediation between teachers and their pupils. Indeed, in schools where classes are large and the average teaching commitment is heavy, it will most likely be the sole regular means of communication *of any sort* between teacher and taught. Recent studies by Douglas Barnes (1969, 1976) and by Colin Harrison and Keith Gardner (1977) provide timely reminders of the fact that what teachers might think of as 'communication' in a normal classroom is actually nothing of the sort: although the teacher may be transmitting, very few pupils will be receiving.

Furthermore, the key assumption underlying 'marking' appears to be that a pupil's subsequent writing will be modified for the better. In practice, this is an unrealistic aim for something so often ill-conceived and more of a pain than a pleasure and it seems that when children eliminate mistakes in their writing this does not apparently follow *directly* from the teacher's drawing attention to them. Who and what, then, is 'marking' for? And how has it come to be such a burdensome yet an integral part of a teacher's daily routine? These are the critical questions to which we address ourselves in what follows.

What teachers do with writing

> The ideal, I presume, might be simply to rate work as satisfactory or unsatisfactory. Certainly I would feel happier so as a teacher: I must hope my life will never depend on my ability to define or defend the difference between B— and C+ — a distinction I have had to make hundreds of times and one that may make a considerable difference to students majoring in the subject.
> Herbert J. Muller (1967)[1]

'Correcting', 'marking', 'grading', 'assessing', 'evaluating' — these are all terms used relatively indiscriminately to describe what most teachers do when they collect in pieces of writing from their classes and the words are familiar to any teacher, primary or secondary. Teachers rarely 'receive' written work from children, which would imply the willing transfer of something produced voluntarily from one special interested party to another. They usually 'collect' or 'take' it in, and both words denote an element of compulsion behind the 'request'. Even if a teacher closes a lesson by saying 'I'd like your books in now, please', the signals are clear enough that non-compliance will be punished in some way. As Douglas Barnes (1976) has pointed out, teachers sometimes have to enforce the apparently

3

tacit agreement between them and their pupils about the place and function of writing in school, and this is one of the 'hidden' ways in which they do it.

Another common gambit is for teachers to disguise their intentions by saying 'I'll have your books in now, if I may, so that I can read what you've written', although perversely they will do nothing of the sort. In fact, it is probable that most pupils can see through this one, because they seem to know intuitively that when teachers say they'll 'read' their work, they don't mean that they'll simply read it from left to right, from beginning to end and make a remark aloud afterwards on how satisfying the experience was — which is what pupils will do — given the opportunity to read each other's efforts. The way teachers define 'reading' is different from the way pupils define it and has more to do with examining and proof-reading than with responsive reading. As a result, pupils interpret teacher behaviour differently from the way the teacher intends it to be understood.

A supposedly sympathetic glance or remark directed at a child writing in class can often trigger an overprotective response in the child, an arm being cradled round the book to prevent any outsider from seeing what is going down and the next minute that same child may be clamouring for the teacher to 'read what I've put, sir'. But even that may not be what the child really wants. It will only take an experienced teacher some thirty seconds, if that, to skim a side of a child's writing, but the teacher who looks at it and returns it within that span of time, will be instantly accused of 'not reading it properly'. What might children mean when they say this?

A teacher's 'reading' is so often accompanied by 'marking' that children have developed disconcerting ploys to deal with this, too. A teacher can be asked directly to 'mark' rather than 'read' a completed piece of work, and then be told off as soon as he or she does so: 'Don't do that, Miss. You spoil it when you write all over it like that.' Nor is it uncommon for, say, less academic pupils to ask for their work to be 'marked' later, 'when we've gone, sir'; as if the whole process of writing thoughts down and having them analysed immediately after-wards were acutely embarrassing or painful.

Naturally, such reactions reflect a particular quality of relationship between teacher and pupils, and there are teachers who will never have encountered them. This could either be because they favour an authoritarian approach even to inter-personal matters and thus keep an acknowledged distance between themselves and their classes, or because they are already working towards securing mutal trust and respect in their classrooms, like the teachers whose activities have recently been described by Mike Torbe (1976). It could also be related to the subject they teach most. Lessons in some subjects provide more opportunities than others for children to comment on the work they've been given. Some readers may feel that the children's remarks quoted above border on the impertinent, but this does not render them any less valid, and strangely enough, although they have all been drawn from a secondary context, a primary teacher might view them more sympathetically than a secondary one would. To illustrate this last point, here is yet another common statement from a pupil writing: 'Don't read it yet. I haven't finished.' In a primary school, that request is most likely to be prompted by a child's unwillingness to be interrupted. In a secondary school it becomes increasingly likely that it would be an attempt to ward off the summary dismissal of writing as inadequate.

We have touched here on two vital issues of concern: the ideas that the atmosphere prevailing in the secondary school may well be less conducive to writing than may generally be appreciated and that pupils may be justified in resisting pressure from some teachers to conceive of writing only within certain narrowly-defined limits.

'Correcting' and 'marking' are often used as though they were interchangeable, but strictly speaking, these words do refer to two separate teacher-activities. When teachers indicate errors, omissions, or possible alterations in the text of what a child has written, then they are 'correcting'. For the younger child this may be done most effectively in talk, but teachers of older pupils tend to write their corrections on or at the side of a child's own writing and many use elaborate codes of symbols and abbreviations as a shorthand way of referring to specific categories of mistakes. 'Marking', on the other hand, although generally understood to include 'correcting' and used widely as a generic term, involves the award of an actual mark for a complete piece of work. In this sense it is a summing-up in numerical terms of a pupil's effort and achievement in respect of work he or she has done.

'Grading', too, is a form of summing-up, of course, and in this case work is awarded a grade or letter, usually from the scale A+ to E—, sometimes accompanied by a rounding-off comment from the teacher but, since by no means all teachers see comment-making as obligatory, marks and grades frequently stand alone.

'Assessing' and 'evaluating' belong to a different conceptual category. Whereas 'correcting', 'marking' and 'grading' all describe what a teacher may do on a day-to-day basis with single pieces of work from each pupil, 'assessing' and 'evaluating' imply a broader view of effort and achievement derived from the inspection of all the work produced by individual children over a reasonable period of time — every month, half-term, term or year. An assessment of performance will probably be recorded on a more formal basis than weekly marks or grades and be available for the whole staff of a department or school to consult. 'Evaluating' similarly connotes the making of long-term judgments on pupils' progress, but perhaps with the more limited objective of acting as a check on the pace that a teacher has set in a block of lessons. Evaluation of learning really seeks to establish whether or not a pupil has grasped a body of knowledge before the teacher attempts to introduce new material.

'Assessing' and 'evaluating' are seen by some teachers today as both fashionable and commendable activities with positive overtones, while 'correcting', 'marking' and 'grading' are currently underrated and viewed negatively. Nevertheless, 'correcting', 'marking' and 'grading' — seen as facets of a total *response* to writing — are vital critical skills which can be used constructively and beneficially in schools and the training of teachers should take far greater account of this than hitherto. Even if one accepts that many teachers over the past century have practised these skills badly, reform lies not in doing away with them altogether, but rather in making them more effective aids to learning. Having said that, of the three, 'correcting' is the skill to which most attention is devoted in this book.

The relationship that can be seen to exist between writing, on the one hand, and correcting on the other, is undeniably flawed. The results of our own investigation suggest that the correction of written work in certain ways acts forcefully as a constraint on pupils to conform to a narrow, counter-productive interpretation of the function of writing. Indeed, it appears that the sort of correction that many teachers practise closes off more possibilities for learning than it opens up.

An analogy may be helpful to clarify this point. If we look at talking rather than writing for a moment, we expect to find a speaker and a listener. Now suppose the speaker has something important to say — a story to tell — or more relevantly for our purposes here, some newly-acquired information to impart. The speaker selects a listener and begins to speak. Imagine, however, that the speaker can make no headway because the listener immediately interrupts to correct the pronunciation of a word or the inflexion of the voice, or to supply a word to carry the speaker over a hesitation. What is more, the listener does this every time a slip of the speaker's tongue is detected. Eventually the speaker abandons the attempt in desperation, having been made to feel thoroughly self-conscious of his or her own inadequacies and having completely lost the drift of what it was he or she wanted to communicate. The listener is deprived of sharing the speaker's particular experience, but the speaker is also deprived because through telling someone else about it, the experience would have, in some way, been made uniquely personal. Rendered literally speechless by the listener's undue attention to the mechanics rather than the meaning of what he or she wanted to say, all the speaker has learnt from the interchange is to play safe in future and not attempt to formulate a coherent utterance on that topic for that listener again.

If school work were predominantly oral in nature and our example were to be set in a school context with the pupil as speaker and the teacher as listener, then given our conditions the pupil would learn very little, except perhaps that adults rate the medium of communication more highly than its content. As Marshall McLuhan (1967) has expressed it, 'societies have always been shaped more by the nature of the media by which men communicate than by the content of the communication'. Since writing actually predominates as the mode of learning in schools today, what we are saying in our analogy is that teachers whose first reaction to children's writing is always to correct it from start to finish are behaving exactly like the pernickety listener. They do not facilitate learning; they inhibit it, and for very much the same reasons. How, therefore, can this danger be avoided?

One significant measure of a pupil's progress in writing is the extent to which the work conveys accurately and accessibly to the reader meanings of ever-changing complexity. Thus, if teachers wish to consider how they should respond to writing, then they must take into account questions of reading and comprehension.

Most teachers consciously try to foster reading for pleasure and for meaning, but less often apply the principles involved to their own reading of pupils' written work. Considering that most adults read a wide variety of fiction and non-fiction *principally for pleasure,* it should not be hard to devise criteria for pupils' writing done in school based on its acceptability as entertainment and instruction. Such criteria should indeed be part of the pupil-writer's awareness of the reader's needs.

As to reading for meaning, we can profitably begin by asking ourselves two questions: what makes a good or a bad reader? and which are we? Colin Harrison and Keith Gardner (1977) suggest that good readers are good because they are *flexible* in their approach to reading. Commenting on an experiment conducted with twelve-year-olds, they make this observation:

> The good readers . . . slowed down their reading when they encountered what they took to be a section which needed closer attention, or perhaps it would be more accurate to say that they allowed more time for reflection between bursts of reading, in order to tease out meanings.
>
> This process of re-reading and reflecting on points in the text which present difficulties or anomalies is absolutely crucial, and yet it needs to be stressed that until very recently the notion of going back and re-reading chunks of text was frowned upon in some circles and by some teachers.

Through investigating the correcting strategies adopted by selected groups of teachers, we have ourselves arrived at a broadly similar conclusion; that a direct relationship exists between a corrector's ability to read a given text flexibly, and his or her capacity for identifying relevant growth points for the writer.

There is one other important aspect of reading for meaning. As the basis of textual analysis and criticism, it has its roots in *comprehension* — defined thus by John Dixon *et al* (1977):

'Comprehension' — of language and of human behaviour — calls for a common-sense or conceptually analytic awareness of what is going on, together with an over-all attitude of standing back and getting its message into perspective. Once this is achieved we can act on the message, responding more intelligently and appropriately. Thus comprehension relates to speech and writing in which we are being informed, advised, warned, persuaded, enlightened, and so on — there is a vast variety, which makes comprehension complex enough without adding in imaginative writing, where an *appreciative* response is primarily called for, and which will involve the reader in imaginative recreation and interpretation of what he reads.

It is this fundamental yet complex activity, then, which should be at the heart of any teacher's response to any child's writing, rather than giving attention solely to the surface features of written language in use. What research evidence there is in this area attests to the soundness of pupils' intuition when they demand that teachers should apply themselves more openly to questions of meaning and style. Barbara Zussman (1975) for example, has interpreted pupils' demands thus: ' "Take the time to explain to us what we are doing or not doing to come up to your standards and we'll try. Otherwise you are just turning us off!" ' If children need guiding through learning processes at school, then such a requirement is not unreasonable. Corrections, marks and grades on their own don't tell students how well they've done, nor what their strengths and weaknesses are, especially if the original task set has involved writing at length, and we should feel moral and professional obligations to respond to genuine effort in an equally genuine way.

Experienced primary teachers have suggested that receiving a mark out of ten for work done is understood and appreciated by younger pupils. It is also likely that it establishes the bad habit of expecting a mark for everything written, so that marks become more sought after than a reader's opinions. If children's critical awareness is diminished like this at an early stage at schooling, then many difficulties are inevitably created for teachers at higher levels of the education system and for the pupils themselves in their struggle to become autonomous writers.

This is not to say we oppose the awarding of marks in appropriate circumstances, namely when both teacher and pupils are agreed beforehand that a finite number of marks may be gained by completing certain specified tasks satisfactorily. There is no doubt that marks *used selectively* can encourage further learning. Say a child is set ten sums to do and having done them and had them marked, she finds she has been given 9 out of 10: by studying the accompanying nine ticks and one cross on her paper, it will not take her long either to see that one answer was wrong or to begin to puzzle out why. Similarly, if a child is tested on ten spellings and gets 7 out of 10, then he can set to work right away to locate and learn the three he got wrong.

But what precisely is right or wrong with a two-side English composition awarded 6 out of 10? And does 6 out of 10 for an English composition signify the same as 6 out of 10 for a piece of writing in history, or geography, or RE — even assuming all those subjects were taught by the one class teacher? And in any of those instances, what would the child have to do to gain 10 out of 10? It is all but impossible to answer any or all of these questions in a straightforward manner. Although it masquerades as an objective operation, the awarding of marks in such cases is actually arbitrary. Furthermore, the practice unhelpfully implies that in order to arrive at their marks teachers read children's work in a highly sophisticated and specialized way, one which children themselves could never begin to understand. In other words, it could generate a confusing image of the relationship between reading and writing at a critical stage of a child's intellectual development.

At first sight, grading offers a teacher more flexibility, its comparative lack of precision often being seen as its saving grace. Yet the very fact that a single grade can be assigned to a broader spectrum of work than a single mark is also the system's greatest weakness. If 6 out of 10 is hard to interpret across the curriculum, it is much more difficult to relate a C+ in history to a C+ in science or English, or to understand what extra effort might have converted C+ to B— or higher. Is the underlying standard that of the pupil's own previous level of attainment, or is it established by a comparison of his or her work with that produced by classmates on that particular occasion? How many pupils have so basic a point explained to them in detail? And how capable are teachers themselves of unravelling such distinctions? Richard Atkinson (1975), for one, has been:

> ... tempted to wonder just how frequently members of a department sit down and discuss the criteria by which they propose to mark the third-year English essays or the second-year History essays. They may well discuss how certain components of their course are to be weighted ... but this is not the same thing. Criteria, therefore, might be explicit or implicit; they might find common utilization within a department or they might not be discussed at all.

Atkinson's point cannot be taken lightly. If a pass/fail concept is additionally built into a marking or grading system, then it is only justifiable if the system itself and its subdivisions can be defended on strictly rational grounds. Thus we move from discussing an apparently simple classroom practice to discussing what constitutes ethical behaviour on the part of a teacher. Of course, genuine doubt about the objectivity of either marks or grades, even at the highest levels of academic study, has existed for many years.[2] Why, then, do so many teachers today still assume that there is special merit in, or right on the side of, one or other system? It is only when marks and grades cease to be regarded as fetishes that they will be used properly, as tools for a known range of specific purposes.

Writing at school: some practical and organizational difficulties

> In school ... it is almost always the teacher who initiates the writing and who does so by defining a writing task with more or less explicitness. Not only does he define the task but also nominates himself as audience. He is not, however, simply a one-man audience but also the sole arbiter, appraiser, grader and judge of the performance. He becomes an audience on whom pupils must focus a special kind of scrutiny in order to detect what they must do to satisfy him. The peculiar feature of this relationship is that the pupil will see his teacher's response as a means by which his progress is being charted. It is part of a larger and more elaborate system of making judgments

11

and not simply a question of the reader's pleasure or insight. Indeed the writer is frequently placed in the position of telling the reader what the latter already knows more fully and more deeply.

James Britton *et al* (1975)

Few of us genuinely appreciate the sheer bulk of writing produced in a school every week, let alone every term or even year. We may suppose that there is a sound educational purpose behind every piece of writing set by teachers for pupils to do, but that may not necessarily be the case. Looking at things pragmatically, all we can say with certainty is that writing is a major activity organized in school which readily fills the time officially set aside for its completion.

Writing a good deal is just as much the norm for most primary children as it so evidently is for secondary pupils and the great achievement of many primary schools has been to nurture the habit of writing with ease and flair about a whole range of topics — so much so that a child can proudly call writing a hobby, and be upset when his class teacher experiments for a week (as this nine-year-old boy's teacher did in 1975) with doing anything but writing:

Last week we were not alowed to rite one single little ful stop for a whole week I did not like it very much becoause I like riting very much it's one of my hobby's at school if we were aloud to rite a little bit I would had liked it a lot but now this week we ar aloud to rite and I am liking that very much. If we were aloud to rite last week I would rite a story and lots more storys.[3]

Unfortunately, the transition to secondary school can bring about a marked change of attitude, as these comments — quoted respectively by Barbara Zussman and Nancy Martin *et al* (1976) — from two older pupils show:

When I get a piece of work back and I think it's good and I get a bad mark I feel like frotiling the teacher.

In secondary school my English came under violent attack by a whole series of teachers . . . The head thought I was dyslectic (never can spell even now). I think I just hated

writting or rather I actually enjoyed writting untill work
was returned to me with such red lines and a poor grade.

So what goes wrong?

There are two main root causes of change at secondary level.
The first, obviously, is the increasing age of the pupils themselves: teachers can do little to compensate for emotional
upheaval at the onset of puberty. The second is the sharp
reduction in the amount of contact between individual teachers
and individual pupils, itself a by-product of the switch from a
single class teacher to a plurality of subject specialists. Even in
the smallest secondary school, the timetable fragments personal
relationships as surely as it fragments knowledge.

The traditional scapegoat is, of course, the examinations
system; yet, in some ways, this is too easy a target, and looking
to the fifth year will not help us to see why writing loses its
appeal so well as looking to the first.

By the end of the primary stage children will have grown
accustomed to producing written work of particular kinds.
They will also have come to expect that it will all be assessed
by one teacher familiar with the overall picture of each child's
written progress. In the first few weeks after transfer, those
same children have several radical adjustments to make which
are critical to their ultimate success or failure in the education
system:

1 The social context in relation to one's peers has to be re-
  defined. The child is a member of a new class, amongst
  strangers.

2 Each child has to memorize and follow a comparatively
  complicated timetable, involving many room changes. (The
  form room may not even be one of the classrooms in which
  the child is taught.)

3 The child has to learn the names of and adapt to the idio-
  syncrasies of some ten or twelve new teachers, for most of
  whom, pupils will have to write more than once a week.

4 The children have to accept that in all probability none of
  the teachers will know anything about them or about the
  work they have done in the past. Nevertheless, they will
  expect them to have reached a certain standard in their
  own subjects. (Liaison between schools is admirable in

13

principle, but there are practical difficulties when secondary schools are served by six or seven contributory schools.)

5 Children can no longer expect the same degree of individual attention and support from each teacher. (*At best* they may be one of well over 100 pupils that any one teacher sees every week, and being in the intake year they will have a low priority by comparison with fifth-year examination candidates.)

6 The pupil must therefore develop a willingness to work more independently, often without the benefit of conversation with either peers or teachers, and to use some of what has hitherto been private time, outside school hours, to complete set assignments.

7 When the children have completed a piece of writing, they must learn that often it will not be read immediately by the teacher who set it. Usually the book in which the writing was done will be taken away at the end of a lesson, as one of a pile of thirty, and be returned some two or three days later — at the earliest. When it is returned, the writing will have been corrected and marked, but different teachers will have done it in different ways. In fact the return of the book may in itself signify the *end* of a particular piece of work, and the writing may never be directly referred to again.

8 The correction and marking of written work may well reflect a concern for the observance of certain abstract conventions rather than originality. Handwriting, layout, even the total number of words produced, will all assume greater significance in the assessment process, together with other 'hidden' factors. Ray Bull and Julia Stevens (1976) suggest, for example, that 'marks given for essay style and general quality plus the overall ability of the writer are those most influenced by the variables of attractiveness, sex of writer and penmanship'. First impressions, in every sense of the phrase, are thus seen to be crucial.

None of these points has any direct bearing upon the secondary school's undisputed function of preparing pupils for examinations. Taken together, however, they ensure that every academic lesson becomes testing in both senses of the word for the children and as a result, pupils' attitudes towards writing in particular can be drastically modified. Yet this is a point surprisingly overlooked in specific studies of children's adjustment to secondary schooling. One of the most recent, by M.B. Youngman and E.A. Lunzer (1977), whilst accepting that new pupils are apprehensive about the more academic nature of secondary education, can only offer 'more familiarization with tests and examinations' *at the primary level* as an inadequate solution to this dimly-perceived problem.

But the secondary school cannot take the entire blame for such aversion; even infant children can come under stress if a teacher reacts poorly to their earliest attempts at *public* writing. Both Nancy Cox (1976) and Nancy Martin (1976) cite clear instances of teachers failing to motivate young pupils who were comparatively fluent writers *at home*, and as they move up through the school system, the problems for such children are undoubtedly accentuated by the teacher's increasing perception of his or her role as being primarily that of examiner.

The nature of writing as a skill (as opposed, say, to talking or drawing) can prove a major stumbling-block to the younger child, too, especially if adults stress too heavily the idea that early progress predicts eventual life-chances. Connie Rosen (1973) had this to say about such conflict as it widely affects primary pupils:

> It is easy to think of many reasons why a young child should not want to write and very difficult to think of reasons why he should . . . Why should he want to put on paper (or via paper) what he can so much more easily say directly? Whatever doubts may be expressed about the curriculum, no one questions that writing should be taught in school; writing, like reading, belongs to school. All parents are concerned about literacy and feel they know whether schools are getting on with the job. And literacy is so obviously marketable and such a clear investment (for the secondary school, for a job, for life), so the argument runs, that inspectors, advisers and even professors of education who have never taught anyone to write share the concern and possibly create some of it. Add to this that writing presents a variety of difficulties at different levels, from the sheer manipulative problems in handling

15

an implement to questions of organization and adjustment to the particular forms of the written language. Small wonder then that teachers, intimately aware of the possibilities of failure and of how manifest that failure is, should be affected to the point of anxiety ... Writing, however much we have come to appreciate content and personal involvement, can be seen to be either accurate or inaccurate, and numerous spelling or punctuation errors in a child's work seem to indicate unmistakable school failure.

Thus pressures from the wider society cannot be discounted, if it is indeed at society's behest that a teacher assumes the role of examiner in the broadest sense. Society's pressures are nevertheless subordinate to those pressures operating within any classroom and we intend to concentrate on the peculiar difficulties writing presents to secondary-school pupils.

Notes

1   Muller, with long experience of the American grade system, is more sensitive than most English commentators to the constraints that the formal assessment of written work imposes upon teachers and pupils alike. The quotation comes from a longer consideration of this problem in his account of the influential Dartmouth Seminar (1966), whereas there is no corresponding discussion to be found in the original English record of the same conference, *Growth Through English* (John Dixon, 1967, Oxford).

2   See, for example, Sir Philip Hartog *et al* (1935):

> There seems to be a fundamental difference between the two systems. The literal system indicates only an order in classification, not ratios of proficiency ... It would appear that the literal mark indicates in the examiner's mind a certain 'quality'. The question of 'quantity' probably enters into his estimate only in a subordinate degree. With the numerical system, on the other hand, the marks for individual questions are added up to furnish a total, a procedure which is convenient, though it is based on hypotheses which it is not perhaps easy to analyse and justify.

More recently (and perhaps more relevantly) it has been suggested in Schools Council Working Paper No 59 (1977) that 'marking in grades seems unhelpful to pupils not yet thirteen' and that it is only of real use in connection with the written output of examination candidates at the upper end of the secondary school.

3   Quoted from *A Week Without Writing*, the contribution of a Coventry primary school class teacher to NATE/doc Pack 5 (July 1975).

2 The reception of one pupil's writing: a case study

Laborious marking by the teacher, even when followed by correction by the student, fails in its object because a disgruntled, disappointed, uninterested and hasty scribbling of a correction is quite insufficient to eradicate an error which is deeply implanted, which was the result of eager and interested endeavour and which has been repeated many dozens of times in writing, in speech in and out of school, and in 'mental trial' before utterance.

F.G. French (1949)

If the characteristic way in which an individual teacher sets pupils writing tasks may be termed *presentation*, then the overall response to the writing when completed may, in the terminology of Douglas Barnes (1971), be referred to as *reception*, 'the teacher's main immediate means of influence':

When a teacher is spoken to by a pupil, or receives a piece of writing, he may reply to it, or comment on it, or assess it and his habitual choice amongst these three will influence his pupils' future uses of language: no one readily embarks upon personal reminiscence when he expects to receive in reply a cool assessment of his delivery. But the teacher's influence is still more pervasive: a snub or bored acceptance, or an interested or enthusiastic reply all have immediate as well as long-term effects. When a criticism is made it can vary both in intensity and in the degree to which it is publicly made.

In a secondary school, however, unfortunately for pupils, great variation in both presentation and reception of such tasks across the curriculum is unavoidable; and as we have already suggested, how teachers deal with mistakes in particular often conflicts with the guidance pupils themselves feel they ought to receive. If the most effective learning does follow on from making mistakes (or at least false starts), then the alienation of so many pupils from the writing process may largely stem from a sense of frustration with teachers who ride roughshod over the gaps in learning that mistakes signify. As Peter Medway (1973) has expressed the predicament, it may well be that the pupil finds 'writing for him serves a function remote from the normal functions of most (familiar) language: one explicable only in terms of the institutionalized procedures of schools, and one irrelevant to his own learning needs'.

But there are not only diametrically opposed views of what constitutes learning at issue: mistakes offend against a teacher's aesthetic sense, too, and the 'copybook approach' to writing in school has been deeply ingrained for years. In 1914, for instance, the Board of Education remarked that the teachers' desire to see 'faultlessly neat and accurate exercises' was leading them to 'restrict unduly the child's efforts in written composition', and observed that:

> . . . some mistakes in grammar or spelling are inevitable in early exercises and the teaching of composition, like that of any other subject, consists not in shielding a child from every danger of mistake, but in enabling him gradually to correct his errors for himself.

Even at that time, it could be seen clearly that the prevailing automatic and indiscriminate approach to correcting and marking was achieving little:

> The essential point . . . must be that the child should understand what is wrong and know how to correct it. This can never be secured if the teacher's revision goes no further than merely marking every mistake, without regard to its relative importance, and handing the exercise back without comment.

Before studying the quality of a child's writing across the curriculum, we must be prepared to differentiate between three main classes of mistakes: first, those to do with the technicalities and conventions of written language in its own right; second, those to do with the register of specific subjects — a class likely to be increasingly in evidence in the secondary school, as Douglas Barnes (1969) and Andrew Wilkinson (1975) have suggested; and third, those to do with a grasp of subject content. It seems that the distinction between the first and third classes is clear enough to many children, who consciously try to avoid making these errors within a single piece of work. Yet teachers only tend to look for one class or another, rarely for all three simultaneously. A fourteen-year-old boy, quoted by Clive Carré and John Head (1974), obviously had no doubts himself about how to examine pupils' work were he to be in his science teacher's shoes: 'when marking a book,' he said, 'I would look for both neat accurate drawings and written work but I would take into consideration the pupil's English ability when marking written work.' Nevertheless, is it strictly feasible for *all* teachers to overtly employ a comparable 'threeway focus' — that is, on presentation, understanding of content *and* linguistic competence — when they read work produced for them under their specialist subject's by-line?

From the Newbolt Report (1921) onwards, numerous attempts have been made to persuade individual teachers, whatever their specialisms, to discharge their full measure of the responsibility a whole staff should exercise over their pupils' language development. Mostly they have met with little success. The Norwood Report (1943) ironically attributed part of the blame for this to the steady increase in the specialist teaching of English, the 'very provision of special periods for English and the concentration of the teaching into the hands of a few' which tempted teachers of other subjects to feel they were 'free to devote themselves to the special needs of their own subject':

> A pupil might then well feel that, since English was the special province of the English teacher, he was not called upon to expend the same effort upon the English of work submitted to other teachers. The further result has been a disposition to regard attention to English as something to be turned on when a specific limited purpose was in view, as, for example, an English essay, or the satisfaction of particular teachers who happened to be 'faddy' about English. English then becomes something to be added or withheld at will and not regarded as inherent and of the greatest moment in all expression of ideas, no matter what the subject.

We have been fortunate to obtain access to a virtually complete record of one boy's written output for the whole of his secondary school career, and thus we have been able to study, year by year, subject by subject, the indicators of progress offered by his teachers' corrections, marks and comments. We have seen the range of mistakes a pupil can make over a five-year period, and we have seen the corresponding range of responses to them. Since the picture is a cumulative one, we have also been able to judge, in terms of the boy's adaptations to criticism, how realistic teachers' expectations of improvement are.

We shall call our selected pupil Michael. As one would expect, Michael's English teachers pay the most attention to technical aspects of his written work. They assume responsibility not only for ensuring that he produces an acceptable amount of writing in relation to his age, but also for seeing that he sets it out neatly. Be this as it may, we should note at once that in his first year his English teacher fights, and loses, the first battle — against the deterioration of his handwriting.

With the benefit of a history exercise book surviving from Michael's last year at junior school, we can see he had previously been directed to use a fountain pen whenever possible, that his use of ball-point for writing compositions was actively discouraged and that at the age of eleven his best writing was done in a bold hand. In short, the foundations had already been laid for a mature style of handwriting to evolve in successive years (p. 21). Yet the majority of Michael's secondary work is written in ball-point, from the very first traditional piece (in which he describes himself, his family and where he lives) onwards. The character of his handwriting starts to disintegrate, so that second-year work (for which he returns briefly to fountain pen) is no longer recognizably that of the same pupil. By the age of sixteen, his style and letter forms are less fluent and accomplished than they were at eleven.

Although a young person's handwriting usually shows marked changes of style in adolescence, penmanship is, as we intimated earlier, one of the critical factors governing the stance which teachers adopt towards pupils' work. First impressions stick; scruffy, poorly written work is generally marked harder than clear, tidy work. (See Briggs, 1970). It is not that legibility is an unrealistic or an undesirable goal, but too often perfectly ordinary work gains unfair credit solely on the grounds of

Vortigen, Hengist and Horsa

Vortigen was a British king who lived in Kent and he did not have an army because the Roman legions had gone to defend Rome the he: he heard that the anglo-saxons were raiding Kent and Suffolk so he decieded that he would ask two anglo-saxons Hengist and Horsa to fight them off and they did so he said you can have as much land as you can cover with cow hide so craftily Hengist and Horsa cut it into strips and covered a lot of ground to build a fort on the island off thannet off the coast of Kent near the Humber (later on he gave them the island) later they wanted more land and money but Vortigen would not let them have it so Hengist and Horsa jioned with the other saxons and took away his kingdom this started the Anglo-saxons invasoin of this contry neatness, as if that were *all* that writing in school was about. Look more closely at what passes for clear, tidy, correct work, and one may well find, in the words of Schools Council Working Paper No 9 (1967), that it is also 'inert, unimaginative, bored and boring' — which is why teachers need to be trained to view all their pupils' efforts more sympathetically:

> ... the marker must be confident enough to give credit for slight evidence. He must, that is, be skilled in critical discrimination and sure of his perceptions so that when he encounters the unusual, even in an undistinguished context, he can see it for what it is.

How Michael's first-year English teacher receives his work is worth closer study, because by taking her place we can re-examine the problem of adapting a new pupil to the accepted norms of secondary education. We come, in effect, to understand how socialization operates at the sharp end. She makes no issue of Michael's handwriting until the second term, by which time, presumably, she has decided it is showing none of the hoped-for signs of improvement. By contrast, her earliest demands arise from his lack of organizational skills and his apparent ignorance of conventions applicable to formal written English.

His first self-introductory composition, half-a-page in length, scores 7/10 and this turns out to be his average mark over the year as a whole. The piece also attracts the single comment 'Paragraphs!' a point Michael steadfastly ignores in nearly every subsequent piece of work. (Nor does the teacher make any further reference to it in the course of the year, although by the end of it Michael still obviously has no idea how to set about paragraphing.)

Six compositions later, she singles out his poor punctuation of a short description of a pole-vaulter in action. Still no longer than half-a-page, this scores 6/10 and the disapproving comment 'All one sentence, and not even a full stop at the end!' This time, however, Michael responds, and his next piece of imaginative writing, 'Fire at Sea', is well received. Although by no means all the necessary full stops have been inserted, most of the capital letters have. What is more, the length has trebled, and the story itself (worth 8/10) is judged to be 'well phrased'.

Then concern with Michael's handwriting and his standard of presentation comes to prominence. 'Good' is the only word the teacher includes amongst her comments which might have any bearing on the quality of the work he produces from the end of November onwards. As we can see from the list that follows, every extended remark made in over two-thirds of the year lays stress on the unpleasant *appearance* of Michael's various efforts:

Good — but keep your work neat.	8/10
Good.	8/10
Good — but do not allow your writing to deteriorate.	8/10
Good. Your writing is deteriorating. You are running your words together.	8/10
This is very poor writing. Please be more careful in future.	7/10
Good.	7/10
Good.	6/10
Very untidy work.	6/10

Nevertheless, there is no indication that the boy was ever advised what to do about it, or even to change his pen, let alone shown how to form and join his letters differently.

In fact, this teacher appears well-meaning but not particularly resourceful. Her efforts to rationalize a dilemma regularly encountered by teachers of first-year secondary pupils — namely, whether to praise originality or criticize the absence of conventional 'surface features' — meet with little success, precisely because she fails to perceive that such a dichotomy is a false one. By adopting a mildly regulative stance towards Michael's work, she clearly feels she is adequately fulfilling her role as a secondary English teacher, but there is no evidence that it has any effect on the boy. Her criticisms are based on her notion of a good adult model for writing: her very first comment ('Paragraphs!') pitches straight in at this unrealistic adult level. The only specific errors she openly takes into account are misspellings and she often writes corrections of these in the margin, yet Michael only once writes out a list of corrections himself (covering mistakes made over a three-month period) and this includes a mistake made by the teacher ('peninsular' instead of 'peninsula', for Michael's 'penisala'). Basically an impression marker, she may do the child-writer a disservice by not communicating her impressions strongly enough to influence the *style* and *content* of his subsequent work.

A regulative approach is also characteristic of Michael's second-year teacher who displays, if anything, a more pronounced concern with standards of neatness and correctness. After each major piece of writing has been completed and checked, he requires comprehensive corrections to be copied out; but if he doesn't explain *why*, at least he explains *how* they should be done, by making the class copy his instructions into their exercise books at the beginning of the year:

1 *Spelling Mistakes* — Write the word correctly *three* times.
2 *Any other sort of Mistake* (Punctuation, words missed out, bad choice of words) — Write the *WHOLE* sentence again.

He too latches on to Michael's handwriting as a significant difficulty, although perhaps he does this more out of a sense of 'professional' indignation than for any justified reason. In English lessons, at any rate, the boy reverts to a fountain pen for the best part of the year (that is, from October to June) and yet his teacher often uses Michael's handwriting as an excuse for denying him excellent marks — notably in the case of a five-page composition entitled 'Invasion from Mars', which scores the hairsplitting mark of 9—/10 and which is deemed to be 'quite good — apart from the difficulty of reading your writing!'

However, because the teacher sustains throughout the year a pattern of written work followed by exhaustive corrections, he succeeds both in forcing Michael to attend to his correcting and marking and in helping him to eliminate many errors of spelling, punctuation and sentence construction. Even faulty paragraphing is overcome in this way. Admittedly, much close work on the teacher's part is required to achieve such encouraging results and red ink is therefore much in evidence; but this example does demonstrate the *positive* aspects of a traditional approach.

A marked contrast with the previous two years is immediately apparent when we look at Michael's third-year English. The ritual of correcting technical errors in detail, of rewriting phrases and sentences accurately, disappears and is seemingly replaced by very little. Yet Michael's powers of self-expression continue to improve. Judgments about the impact of this change on Michael's work and progress must be tentative, however, since there are comments from more than one teacher in the relevant exercise book. It would appear that Michael was taught English by one, or possibly two students on teaching practice in the course of the year and the regular teaching of his class seems to have been shared anyway. Under these circumstances, what is of general interest is that all the various comments incline towards a more supportive relationship between reader and writer.

Here are some of the more striking assessments made of Michael's creativity and style at this period:

(a) in response to the second half of a long composition entitled 'Hijacked', in which he proposed a new method of foiling hijack attempts —
    8/10. Incredibly complex and original suggestions. Good thinking though I doubt if it could work in practice. What happens when the plane arrives at the airport to find it blocked by snow or fog?
(b) in response to a composition entitled 'The Battle of Broad Close' —
    8/10. I like your description of this 'battle' it makes it sound like the real thing.
(c) in response to a short criticism of a mail-order advertisement —
    7/10. Also, is it 'sensational and new'?
(d) in response to a story about a fighter pilot, 'James Tubb'—
    8/10. Good, exciting rubbish. Suitable for a 'comic'.
(e) in response to a description of 'The Apollo 14 Splashdown' —
    8/10. Good. Be careful your sentences do not become too similar in their construction. Restrict your use of commas.
(f) in response to a comprehension exercise, 'Phoenix Victor Mike' —
    8/20. So what! Your ideas aren't bad but you have not put them over clearly.

All the adults who made these remarks had at least one thing in common of some value to Michael: in the main, they let his work stand unaltered, because they wanted to show him that above all else they had read carefully and reflected upon what he had written. In view of the low incidence of mistakes and an increased output over the year, it appears this was the sort of guidance Michael genuinely appreciated.

To complete the picture of his English performance, we must turn briefly to Michael's fourth- and fifth-year books. They show a more clearly defined and specialized course of tuition in progress, as he prepares for O Level Language and Literature, as well as giving us some idea of the cumulative effect of having a single teacher for two consecutive years.

In earlier books there is no sign of writing for the purpose of literary criticism, but in these last two years this type of work predominates, and Michael's first fourth-year piece about 'Yorkshire Schools in Dickens' Day' is very different from anything he has been set to write before. As time goes by, we see him writing confidently about the character of Rosalind in *As You Like It*, or the significance of the letter from Mr Darcy to Elizabeth Bennet in *Pride and Prejudice*; and thus the child's composition is superseded by the young student's essay.

During this important transitional stage, indirect help comes in the guise of other, apparently unrelated written tasks. By regularly having to answer complicated comprehension questions, Michael's critical use of language is extended, while flexibility of style is encouraged by exercises requiring him to answer the supposed needs of certain specified audiences. (He has, for example, to concoct an estate agent's specification for his school, and a few weeks later he is writing 'A Play for the Theatre in the Nineteenth Century'.) Transfer of training evidently occurs: in his last major fourth-year piece, Michael shows he is capable of integrating a variety of writing skills by producing some five-and-a-half pages of what his teacher rightly calls 'detailed and sensitive analysis' based on an extract from *The Hound of the Baskervilles*.

In the fifth year there are signs of a much tighter control being exerted, as the teacher attempts to initiate more of a critical dialogue with Michael in the interests of 'examination technique'. Hence lengthy comments, marginal notes and questions abound; but ironically, the year in which the greatest demands are made upon him is also the year in which Michael makes the greatest number of mistakes, so there are masses of specific corrections too. The onus therefore falls more and more on Michael to match his whole approach to the undisclosed, yet clearly perceived adult model set up inside his teacher's head. In itself, this illustrates a prime difficulty from the boy's point of view: when does his role as a potential adult take precedence over his more familiar role as pupil-writer? Playing at being a writer is hard, despite the experience which Michael may have gained in this lower down the school, but having to pretend to be an adult before his time is having to play a game on unfair terms, since he can never make the full imaginative leap necessary to achieve success. In fifth-year English the two roles frequently overlap, so if we find many mistakes being made at this level, we must ask ourselves how well the teacher has fitted his pupil to construct *in his imagination* a situation for writing he may not have encountered in reality.

Reflection on this point, which opens up a dimension missing from standard notions of 'correctness', is important. Consider, therefore, the teacher's response to the outcome of an extraordinary exercise Michael was set towards the end of his fifth year — to imagine he was a nervous traveller leaving the country by air, who was making his will before take-off (p. 28):

> 7/10. Quite good attempt.
> A somewhat rushed job!
> If you expect such excellent service you should be more specific in your instructions — otherwise your solicitor will have to waste a good deal of time looking up names, addresses etc.

In other subjects with a heavy writing requirement for pupils (history, geography, and the sciences), Michael's teachers adopt the traditional, stereotyped approach of reading and marking his work for content, not style. In addition, very few spelling corrections are made, either of mistakes in common words ('differance' persists throughout Michael's first-year geography) or, more unexpectedly, of those made in technical terms, e.g.: 'mirandering water coarse' (geography), 'oxsiding' and 'oxsidising' (chemistry). In part, this can be explained by the fact that the nature of much of the written work given in these subjects theoretically precludes the possibility of mistakes occurring. Notes taken down from dictation, tasks set from course-books, and periodic tests calling only for short answers seem to make up the bulk of such work, in fact.

There are few equivalents to the comparatively regular compositions set by Michael's various English teachers. When

Dear Mr. Bailey,

I shall be leaving the country for Iran tommorow evening. I feel the need to make this will before I leave, due to recent air disasters and trouble in the bordering countries.

To my eldest son I leave my house and all its furniture, the key to my prive beareau and an equal share of my premium bonds, stocks and shares. The Mercedes I leave to my eldest daughter. All my money is to be shared equally amongst the other three and any in excess of the value of the car and house shall be shared amongst all five. My shares and premium bonds shall be shared between all five and my business in town I leave to my youngest son.

My collection of diamonds I leave to my youngest daughter and any other jewels or precious stones I leave to my daughter Jane. The two motorcycles in my possession I leave to my youngest son also, provided he does not sell the vintage model. If this is his intent it must be given to the museum.

Finally my beloved dog I leave to my youngest daughter.

The arrangement for the witnessing of this will must be made before 6 p.m tommorow evening, because it is at this time I depart for London airport.

28

such pieces are forthcoming, however, style is usually seen as a pre-packaged component that can be built into the work at will — exactly in keeping, of course, with the fears expressed thirty-six years ago in the Norwood Report. Hence Michael's second-year history teacher sees the marginal remark 'Badly expressed' as adequate comment on the confusion apparent in the following sentence:

> When he took a scutage from a knight, which was payment instead of raising an army and fighting for him, he often took twice a year instead of the maximum, which was once a year.

His science teachers, on the other hand, tend to take a far more forceful line. Spelling and punctuation do not specially concern them, but they are clearly disturbed by poor presentation or evidence of illogical thought-processes. In extreme cases, their habitually lengthy comments amount to lecturettes promoting the virtues of their own subjects, although they still acknowledge the need for what Peter Doughty (1968) labelled 'INTELLIGENT ENGLISH that is both ACCURATE and LOGICAL':

5/10.   Science must concern cause & effect.
       Just to describe effects is hardly science.
       You *must* spend more time assembling your ideas, arranging them & then *choosing* the best possible words to express them.
D.   What about the word CLONE?
       You could do much better.

These remarks appended to a third-year biology essay on 'Embryology' are heavily value-loaded (pp.30–31). But notice also the confused impression which they give as a whole. Having awarded a *mark* before he begins to write anything, the teacher gives the word a poor *grade* lower down the page. As to the capitalized word CLONE, where might Michael have included it in his original draft? How would he be expected to use it correctly in a sentence? The teacher gives him no clues; and yet his parting shot 'You could do much better' appears to be related to this specific oversight or omission on Michael's part.

EMBRYOLOGY

Biologists have taken [embryos which
have started cell division. In the
embryo, in the larger cells, they have
taken, from the gap which will form
from the intestinal lining of a frog
the intestine,] one separate cell. Then
they have taken an unfertilised egg
from a pond. With these they have
taken (our) the nucleus of each. The
one from the intestine is diploid and
the other is monoploid. They have
then taken the first cell nucleus
and put it in place of the other. ✓

   This first nucleus begins
to develop and divide, feeding upon
material inside the black ovum
the jelly the original cell would have
if it had been fertilised. [This
is because the first cell was diploid,
because the embryo had been fertilised
therefore the cell had to divide
already.] The other cell was monoploid ✓
because it had not been fertilised

30

and cell division ~~had not get begun~~ doesn't take place in unfertilised eggs.

Biologists also found if they took more than one cell from the intestine and used the same process as before all the baby frogs which are produced are identical in every respect. _because_

Floating and Sinking   21/1/70

If a body is placed in a liquid it receives an upthrust from the liquid and its weight seems less.

Imagine a certain volume of the liquid in the liquid.

For example

It is stationary in the liquid, so the upthrust on it is just equal to its weight.

Now imagine that volume of liquid to be replaced by a body of exactly equal shape, such as a stone, a fish, or a boat. This body will receive the same upthrust as the "displaced" liquid did.

So " A body placed in a liquid receives an upthrust equal to the weight of liquid displaced".

If the body weighs more than the liquid it displaces, it sinks. If a body is denser than a liquid it sinks into.

Weight of Empty Beaker. 140.62 grams.

Weight of Metal Cylinder in Air. 76.02 g.

"   "   "   "   " Water 55.9 g.

Upthrust on Cylinder 20.3 grams.

Weight of Beaker & Displaced Water 164.0 gm.

Weight of Water Displaced 23.4 grams.

1) A piece of wood floats because it is less dense than water and it has in it pores and cracks which trap air inside them. A stone sinks because is more dense than the water and it has no pores or cracks. Also the upthrust of the water is not great enough to hold it up.

2) A ship stays afloat because it has air trapped inside, it and for the water to come in and sink it the air must find a way out before the water can come in.

① The particles of wood are less dense than water.

② But why does the air make a difference? What if the ship was empty — a vacuum instead of air; would it float?

(? / 0)

Why is this homework so much like D Bird's?

A boat sinks lower in the water the more it is loaded because the upthrust is still the same but the weight of the boat becomes greater and the upthrust is not able hold the boat up as high in the water because of this.

→ I won't accept this work please repeat this part of the homework. Put the date and "Homework", think about the question and write your answers in properly constructed sentences.

33

Another interesting example of a science specialist's attitude to language and learning can be found in Michael's second-year general science book. As an elementary piece of physics homework, the boy has been asked to write about 'Floating and Sinking'. The teacher, however, has noticed that two important points have been left out, so provides relevant footnotes (excellent responses in themselves) to cover them, as follows (pp. 32—33):

1 The particles of wood are less dense than water.
2 But why does the air make a difference?
   What if the ship was empty — a vacuum instead of air; would it float?

After this attempt to extend Michael's grasp of the set topic, we might expect the teacher to sign off — but no. It strikes him that part of the homework is already familiar to him, being virtually identical to that handed in by another pupil in the same class 'Why is this homework so much like P.B . . .'s?' and he closes the traffic of ideas abruptly and aggressively:

I won't accept this work. Please repeat this part of the homework. Put the date and 'Homework', think about the question and write your answer in properly constructed sentences.

Nevertheless, this teacher's response is as nothing compared to the striking bluntness favoured by his chemistry colleague who teaches Michael in the fifth year. 'So what?' he retorts to a description of the reaction of concentrated nitric acid with tin ('This effervesces and a choking gas is given off'); while that of its effect on lead ('This effervesces slightly and no characterization can be placed on the gas') is dismissed as 'rot'.

A still more fascinating use of written English by a teacher to regulate Michael's own written performance came to light when we examined his fifth-year French book. A French exercise is probably one of the most intensively corrected pieces of work to be found in a secondary school; the explanation, emerging from discussions with modern linguists, being that such close attention to detail is a necessary evil, part and parcel of the fact that there is so much for a pupil to learn (especially for examinations), yet so little time in which to do it. Nor should it be forgotten that an able pupil, with 'a gift for languages', may already possess the necessary drive to be capable of responding positively to frequent correction. Of great interest to us was the discovery that Michael had once had such a 'gift', and that he had been second in his class in French immediately prior to leaving junior school; on the strength of his secondary work, he shows only average aptitude for the subject.

Indeed, his early secondary exercises in French suggest a lack of feeling for the language, an inability to immerse himself in a foreign idiom: often one feels he is doing no more than operating at the level of the helpless tourist, lifting words directly from phrase-book or pocket dictionary.

Notwithstanding this poor showing lower down the school, because he is a boy of above-average ability in overall terms, Michael finds himself working towards an examination in French in his fifth year — under the direction of the same teacher for the third year in succession.

In this instance it is essential to highlight the continuity of teaching, since there was a personality clash between Michael and this particular member of staff. Their dislike of each other was mutual — a problem encountered commonly enough in schools, but less often documented in research. James Britton (1975) has reminded us that:

> while class sizes remain stubbornly at their present level, writing has to stand in for a great deal of interpersonal speech. There will be many children whose relations with their teacher have to be established and maintained principally by what each writes for the other.

The example we are about to examine, (pp.36—37) in which a teacher-pupil relationship established and maintained in the written mode is a bad one, is consequently of some significance, and should prompt the question: how can a teacher avoid his or her use of language falling into a predictably negative, non-productive pattern?

From the volume of red ink he uses alone, it is obvious that this teacher is meticulous about correctness. He is a perfectionist, but one with a problem on his hands — a fifth-year pupil whose linguistic competence in French is way below his own. He adopts a twofold strategy to remedy the situation, correcting every mistake Michael makes and insisting on those corrections being copied out after each new piece of work has been checked;

En Panne   30/3/73

Mon père a levé le capot et a regardé

l̶e̶(a) moteur. Deux d̶a̶ des ̶c̶h̶a̶n̶d̶e̶l̶l̶e̶s̶ ̶é̶t̶a̶n̶c̶e̶l̶l̶e (bougies)

étaient
e̶s̶t̶ cassée̶s̶. Il a fermé le capot et s'est rentré

dans la voiture, mais en vérif̶i̶a̶n̶t̶ (ant) le moteur

ses mains étaient couvertes d'huile.

Après avoir essuyânt(é) (les) ses mains il a dit

"I̶l̶ Ç'est nécessaire de ̶m̶e̶ ̶f̶a̶i̶s̶ ̶u̶n̶ ̶p̶r̶o̶m̶e̶n̶a̶d̶e̶
                        et d'aller au
quitter ̶d̶e̶ la voiture, ̶e̶n̶ ̶r̶o̶u̶t̶e̶, ̶e̶n̶ ̶l̶e̶ prem̶i̶er

garage." Donc il s̶â̶(est)a mis en route et

bientôt il a disparu.

Une heure plus tard il est reveni̶o̶(u) avec

2

                                              (hard)
un air content et une petite boîte Il avait

                      bougies
réussi à acheter des ̶c̶h̶a̶n̶d̶e̶l̶l̶e̶s̶ ̶é̶t̶a̶n̶c̶e̶l̶l̶e̶
            ouvert
à ̶d̶'un garage ̶d̶e̶ vingt-quatre heures. En

peu de
~~pé~~ temps il a remplacé les deux ~~chandelles~~ bougies

~~chandelle~~ et il a mis en marche. le moteur Maintenant

Tense!
nous sommes prêts ~~de~~ à ~~(départe)~~ partir. Mais avant

de partir nous avons vérifiés les pneus,

l'essence et le niveau d'huile.

Nous ~~se~~ nous sommes dirigés vers Oxford

pleuvait
et quand nous avons arrivé ~~il~~ ~~faie plu~~. Mon

fait marcher
père a ~~allumé~~ les essuie-glaces. ~~Par le~~

Quand   Tense
~~temps~~ nous avons arrivés à Campden il est

la pluie
sept heures ~~der~~ matin et ~~le plu est~~ s'arrêtée

Cinq minutes plus tard nous avons arrivés à

Weston et en ~~dix~~ minutes nous étaient tous

endormis. [181 WORDS]

but it fails. The ultimate effect of his dissatisfaction (manifest in the comments shown below in chronological order) is to turn the boy off French altogether:

(a) What a mess your verbs are in!
  Do something about it *now*!
(b) More careful.
(c) Re-write.
(d) Better, but still lots of work to do on verbs.
(e) Verbs still too careless.
(f) See me.
(g) Much more careful. Revise verbs with être, and perfect tense.
(h) Now write était 20 times. (This instruction followed nearly a page of corrections Michael had already done.)
(i) *Much* more thoughtful — but you must check tenses.
(j) Quite good. Do every single correction. (On this occasion there were approximately 50 to do.)
(k) Don't you recognize the perfect, ont + past part?
(l) Not good enough.
(m) Read this through and see where you can use an infinitive — do you see?
  Why are all your verb endings wrong? — start learning what they mean. (Compare this with the despairing tone of a comment written on a fourth year exercise: "Why the -ent ending after 'je'? — because it's *wrong*.")
(n) There is some hope here but you must:
  1) Not make up phrases by using English expressions
  2) Do *all* corrections
  3) Write me a list of *all* verbs which take "être" in the perfect apart from reflexives.
(o) Use an infinitive after de, à etc.
  (as you learned the other day)

As the year goes on, so the demands pile up and up. The overall picture is so black that the unwitting irony of a remark like 'as you learned the other day' is doublethink of a high order: Michael may have been *taught*, or simply *shown* a particular rule, but clearly he didn't *learn* it at all.

Eventually, having done some homework so poorly that at least two errors have been found in every one of its seventeen lines, Michael decides enough is enough and underneath he writes in pencil 'Corrections will appear in this space at a later date'. In fact, he never keeps the promise, ground down by what we might describe as his teacher's 'overkill' strategy.

As we have suggested, this example usefully illustrates one highly specialized aspect of the *teacher's* understanding of what language for learning entails and it is probably the best from all those we have cited by which to judge the effectiveness of a teacher's mistake-handling techniques. Since French is not our everyday adult language, we must assess the value of the corrections and comments much as Michael had to, and the difficulties we may experience in relating them to mistakes occurring in an imperfectly comprehended context should enlighten us.

Although there are areas of the curriculum we have not touched upon here, the overwhelming impression gained from studying Michael's work as we have done is one of variable standards *within* subjects year by year, as well as *between* them and the majority of problems existing both for pupil and teachers are firmly and undeniably rooted *in the use of language*. Consider, for instance, the tension and conflict generated by Michael's history teacher's frequent use of the adjective 'concise' in his summings-up at a time when his English teacher is encouraging him to increase his word-output; or by the same teacher's award of *lower* marks to an essay he rates as 'excellent' than to one he describes as a 'very good effort'.

If anything, the picture assembled in this chapter brings new meaning to the account of Man's use of words provided recently by the Inspectorate (1977), and certainly casts excusable doubt on their assumption that teachers themselves can readily exercise linguistic restraint in the interests of furthering their pupils' understanding:

> . . . we need to select examples that tell pupils, appropriately to their age and experience, what use man makes of words. He tells in different ways what he has seen and done, he gives orders, he formulates opinions and gives reasons, he enters the thoughts and feelings of others, he hurts and assuages, he creates understanding and misunderstanding. These are some of the uses of language that pupils will encounter themselves. In asking pupils to use language, again in ways appropriate to their age and experience, a

teacher has a particular function. He needs to specify the kind of use, for whom it is intended and its purpose. He may need to tolerate, and to expect tolerance of, degrees of hesitancy and uncertainty in language, and to encourage cooperative work with it. At the same time, he needs to prepare for linguistic intolerance, and for attitudes to language which may conflict with those which he is encouraging.

Michael's total school experience of writing is now before us, and so is his experience of his teachers' writing. If we ask, in the DES's words, if his teachers have helped him to refine his use of language by helping him to see the 'kind of use, for whom it is intended and its purpose'; if we look for the 'tolerance of hesitancy and uncertainty'; if we inspect the 'attitudes to language' which the teachers demonstrate in their working — then we end up by asking, what is it that Michael has learnt from his five years of writing? The answer is that what he writes will consistently be inspected for flaws, and will rarely be praised. Furthermore it is probable that Michael's attitude to writing will be that it is a chore and dangerous in the way it makes him vulnerable to attack. What he thinks and feels is apparently unimportant to his teachers. If this is all that he has learned in five years, one wonders if it was worth it.

3 Investigating correcting strategies

As regards correction by the teacher, Senior and Junior School will no doubt agree upon a code of correction for elementary mistakes. Correction should be progressive; the existence of a mistake in a line could be indicated by some mark, but the child could be left to find it out for himself. Above all, attention should not be confined to elementary blunders. The rewriting of a badly formed sentence may be more important still, and constructive criticism, alternative suggestions for wording, and so on, should be given. The teacher, again, might mark the exercises at different times for different purposes, the purpose being made clear to the class when the exercises are given back.

It is fully realised that this more thorough and constructive type of correction will impose a heavy burden on the teacher of a large class. This burden might to some extent be mitigated by more class discussion of the composition exercises themselves, and, possibly, through arrangement with other teachers, by fewer and shorter exercises being written in the time specifically allotted to English. But the whole matter must be regarded as a major problem of school work and organization, and one that is well worthy of investigation over a wide field.

Board of Education (1937)

Having considered the general impression made upon one pupil by his teachers' reception of his written work across the curriculum and having concentrated our attention principally on the likely impact of the comments on that work, we need to examine in greater depth the way individual teachers mark and the potential of their strategies. The narrowing of the focus of our study in this chapter is therefore an attempt to relate specific and characteristic features of a teacher's written performance to the way in which pupils learn to refine their own use of written language.

41

Our first investigation in this field was conducted with the cooperation of the staff of a large 11–18 secondary school. A representative sample of teachers was chosen[1] and asked to correct an identical script, an extract from an imaginative composition written as part of his normal English classwork by a second-year boy at the school. (See Test Script 1: *20 million miles to Earth*.) Information from the completed scripts was then transferred to analysis sheets to identify and compare the various correcting symbols and abbreviations used. (See Fig. 1 p. 43.)

Two main, interrelated purposes lay behind this exercise. The first was to discover how much common ground (if any) existed *in the use of symbols* between members of the same staff trained in different disciplines. The second was to examine the hierarchies of mistakes established by what each teacher chose to correct or ignore.

A further subsidiary aim was to compare the correcting strategies of English specialists with those of other teachers, in the light of evidence from the Bullock Committee's national survey of schools as to the high proportion of non-specialists teaching English at secondary level and by so doing, to assess roughly how far conflicting notions of linguistic competence might affect pupils' progress in written English. In this connection, it should be remembered that no less than 32.8 per cent of English teachers had no qualifications in the subject at the time of the Bullock survey, and other relevant findings were summarized as follows:

> . . . a third of those involved in English teaching have no discernible qualification for the role. Of course, many of these may well be teaching English to only one or two classes, spending most of their time in some other subject. But this in itself is a significant feature and another disquieting aspect of the situation. Of the teachers engaged in English, only 37 per cent spent all their time on it, 25 per cent were teaching it more than half their time, and 38 per cent less than half . . . There can be no other secondary school subject which is staffed by such a large proportion of people without appropriate qualifications. Nor can there be any subject which 'borrows' so many teachers from other areas of the curriculum and assumes they can fill the role with little or no preparation.

20 million miles to Earth.

Now the boy which was in the boat was playing near the sea when he saw the object. He picked it up and took it in a small rocky cave he opened it and saw what was inside it. Then he took it to a man named Dr. Victor the boy sold it for 10 $. Then the Doctor opened it and held it in his hand. To him so that he was dreaming and saw nothing like that in his life before. He lefted it on the table in 2 hour it hached out and inside was a 4" animal it was like a dinorsour. When the Doctor came back he saw it he then picked it up and placed it in a cage.

Now the police was worried and, the next day the doctor got up. He walked to the cage and to his astonment the animal grew up to a man's height. The Doctor knew why it had grew to a man's height in a day it was because when the animal was breathing Carbon dioxide he grow bigger. The doctor immediatly went to the police and told what had happened.

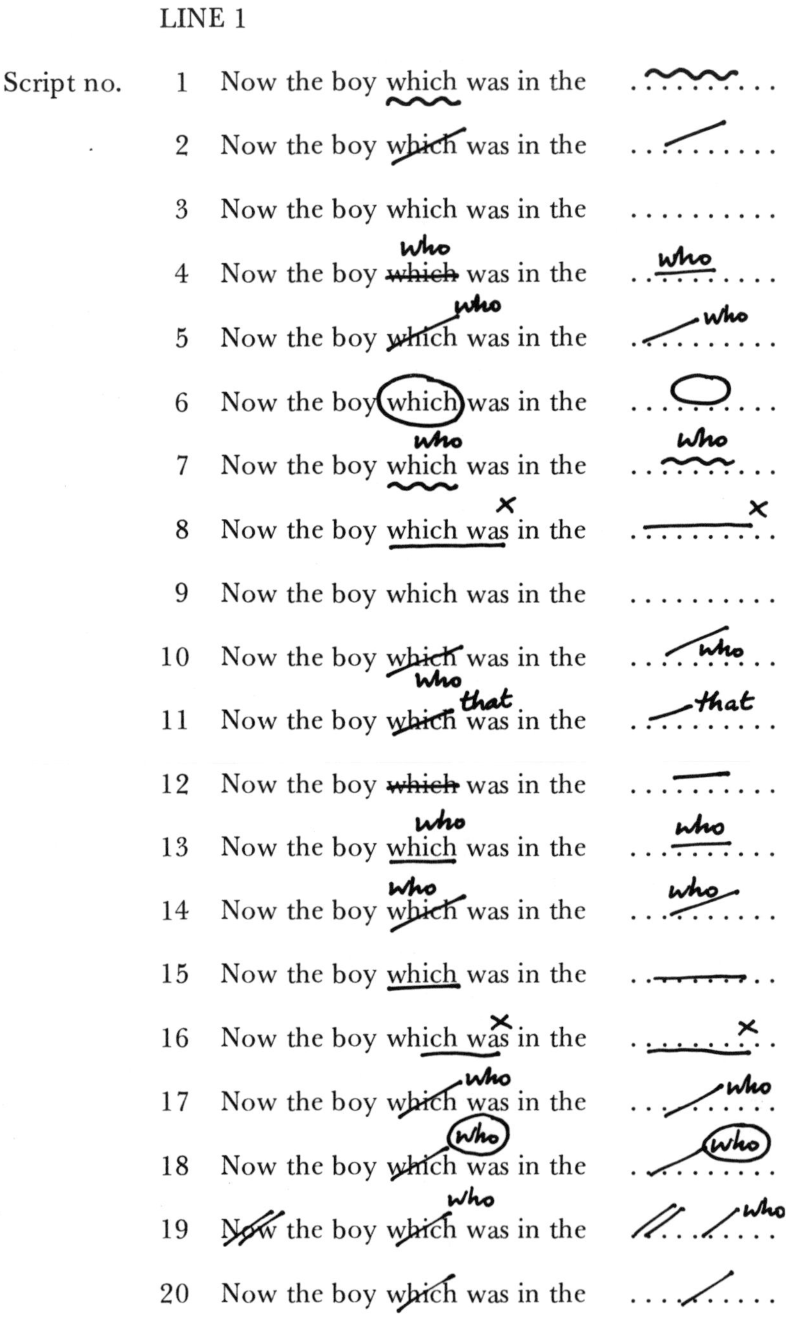

LINE 1

Script no.	1	Now the boy which was in the	～～～...
	2	Now the boy which was in the	.⟋...
	3	Now the boy which was in the	....
	4	Now the boy ~~which~~ *who* was in the	..*who*....
	5	Now the boy which *who* was in the	.⟋ *who*
	6	Now the boy ⟨which⟩ was in the	...◯...
	7	Now the boy which *who* was in the	...*Who* ～～...
	8	Now the boy which was in the ✗	.⎯⎯✗..
	9	Now the boy which was in the	....
	10	Now the boy which *who* was in the	...⟋*who*..
	11	Now the boy which *that* was in the	.⟋*that*
	12	Now the boy ~~which~~ was in the	..⎯⎯.
	13	Now the boy which *who* was in the	...⎯⎯*who*....
	14	Now the boy which *who* was in the	..⟋*who*.
	15	Now the boy which was in the	.⟶..
	16	Now the boy which was ✗ in the	.......✗..
	17	Now the boy which was *who* in the	...⟋*who*.
	18	Now the boy which was ⟨*who*⟩ in the	.⟋... ⟨*who*⟩
	19	Now the boy which was *who* in the	⫽...⟋*who*
	20	Now the boy which was in the	...⟋..

Fig. 1: Specimen analysis sheet.

44

We hoped to examine the implications of this situation in our investigation, and this explains the choice of test script, which typifies the kind of composition secondary English specialists receive constantly — seemingly original in conception, yet technically far from perfect. (We say 'seemingly original', because in the case of this script we did not discover, until later, that the storyline was fairly accurately based upon a film shown on television. This revelation in no way invalidates our findings, but since it came *after* the teachers had corrected their copies of the script, it may indicate how deceptive the 'originality' of children's imaginative writing can sometimes be.)

Before looking in close detail at the outcome of this experiment, however, it is necessary to comment on one significant factor emerging from the circumstances of its administration. Each teacher invited to participate was approached in as informal and relaxed a way as possible, to allay any undue fears, but beyond being told the pupil-writer's age, they were given no further guidance, to ensure some kind of comparability for the results. Yet there was a good deal of probing for more background information, particularly about the boy's supposed ability-level, and several participants declared themselves unable to correct the script without knowing more. This reluctance to proceed after only a minimal briefing, noted also by other researchers into marking, may perhaps have had its roots in a fundamental suspicion of educational research; although it is more likely attributable to the conditioning effect of the school's own internal structure, which was based on broad banding, through which pupils came to be thought of principally in terms of performance.

In terms of raw results, it is the teachers' prolific correction of misspellings that invites the closest attention. Indeed, one such mistake — 'dinorsour' (line 15) — proved to be the most corrected of all in the entire script. Whilst unremarkable in itself (since the mistake is so obvious), this example is more noteworthy in view of the fact that out of a total of twenty-seven, no fewer than sixteen teachers used perceptibly different symbols to correct it. (See Fig. 2 p.46).

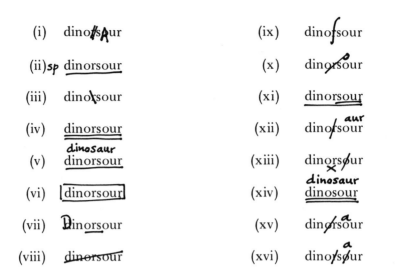

Fig. 2: Corrections of a misspelling.

Item (ii) in our list incorporates the predictable abbreviation 'sp', short for 'spelling' or sometimes 'spelling mistake', which is readily understood by any literate adult and has stood the test of time. Nevertheless, from a child's viewpoint, it may appear unsympathetic, even uncompromising, as it highlights a problem without offering any solution. This may equally be true of the more abstract lines used by the teachers who did not attempt to put the spelling right on the page. Undoubtedly the most striking of these is the complete box round the word — item (vi); yet double underlining — as in items (iv) and (xi) — also falls into the same category. Most negative of all, however, must be the diagonal line straight through the word, as in item (viii).

The remaining alternatives, by contrast, offer positive help of some kind to the writer. Whilst there are only two instances of the word being completely rewritten — items (v) and (xiv) — there are several attempts to show that the first 'r' is superfluous and that the second 'o' should be an 'a' though only four indicated both. However, items (ix), (x) and (xiii) require separate comment, in view of the inadequate symbolism employed in these cases. The strokes in (ix) and (x) are markedly idiosyncratic and strangely distracting, whilst the cross in (xiii) is downright misleading.

46

For the purposes of demonstrating wide discrepancies between the correcting practices of individual teachers within the same school, a better illustration could hardly have presented itself. So many of the sixteen variations we found demonstrably fail to communicate how the word should be spelt and yet with 'dinorsour', the spelling we have shows the writer already has a fair grasp of how to transpose phonics into graphics. Despite two misrepresentations of its component vowel sounds, the basic structure of the word is complete. But if we turn now to 'lefted', an ambiguous misspelling from line 12, we find a different order of problem. (See Fig. 3 below.)

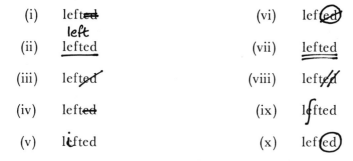

Fig. 3: Resolution of ambiguity in misspelling.

The strokes made through or around this word must stress either the teacher's acceptance or rejection of the writer's *meaning.* In other words, they must be specifically related to the context in which the mistake occurs. Study of our ten examples reveals that most of our sample took the boy to have meant 'left'. On this assumption, the corrected sentence should thus read 'He left it on the table ...', and the action to be taken appears straightforward — to scrub out the '-ed', as shown in items (i), (iii), (iv) and (viii).

Nevertheless, to do this is not to fully identify the problem which the word has set the teacher, nor does it therefore allow the writer to reflect on the possibility of a problem existing. Seen in this light, item (ii) is, at first sight, appealingly simple and direct. Having written 'left' above the pupil's 'lefted', this teacher is enabling him to compare the shape and structure of both words, and to see why the last two letters of his word are superfluous. Yet looking back for a moment at correction (v) of 'dinorsour' should give us pause for thought, since the comparison shows us identical symbolism in use to cover two qualitatively different orders of mistake. Although item (ii) signals the mismatch between the unacceptable and the accepted forms of the verb in question, what it cannot do is indicate that 'lefted' is the result of the writer's response to a miscue.

Those teachers who interpreted 'lefted' as a simple misspelling of 'lifted' — as in items (v) and (ix) — may, of course, have been unaware of any deeper difficulty to explore. Alternatively, they may have mentally acknowledged one, yet still felt the immediate context demanded 'lifted' in preference to 'left'. Only item (v) can be unequivocally construed as indicative of this outlook: (ix) merely hints at it in the unhelpful way already seen elsewhere. (See Fig. 2, item (ix).) As for the teacher offering item (vii) as a correction, which side of the contextual fence is he on? Neither we nor the writer have any way of knowing.

The serious teaching point to be drawn from our criticism of the responses to this error is that there is a range of mistakes in children's writing, of deceptive simplicity, which should not (and which properly *cannot*) be handled by some form of correcting notation alone. Such a conclusion is reinforced by considering the treatment of a more obscure ambiguity in line 10, where the writer's sentence — or thought-structure is inadequate. (See Fig. 4 p.49).

The full stop and the capital 'T' of 'To' are declarations of the writer's intention to begin a new sentence, but in reading on to the next full stop (in line 12) we have in fact scanned a garbled non-sentence and correction of this fault on the page is likely to prove time-consuming, if not futile. Our sample of teachers fretted away manfully at these three lines of the script, and particularly at the initial 'To', but to little avail. Those who did not underline them and write a querulous 'Meaning?' somewhere tried to offer possible subjects and main verbs, so that the omission itself disappeared beneath waves of teachers' writing. This solution circumvents the obvious question: why is there a gap in the logical flow of the story at this point and how had the boy intended to fill it originally? The answer, of course, should be found by asking the writer himself, not by inspired guesswork.

The lack of clear purpose shown by many of the teachers in this instance, perhaps, shows the uncertainty with which they corrected the composition as a whole and suggests they were unable to take the supposed learning needs of the writer sufficiently into account. It would seem reasonable to expect

LINE 10

Script no.

1	his hand‖To him so that he was	. . . .‖. . . . . . .
2	his hand *close* To him so that he was	. . . . .*close to*. . . . .
3	his hand(To him so that he was	. . . .(. . . . .
4	his hand To him so that he was??	??. . . . .??
5	his hand(To him so that he was	. . . . . . ⤨ . . . . .
6	his hand To him so that he was	. . ∼∼∼∼∼∼ . .
7	his hand To him?so that he was	. .∼∼∼?∼∼∼. .
8	his hand To him so that he was	. . . .
9	his hand To him so that he was	. . . .
10	his hand To him *it seemed* so that he was	. . . . .↗.*it seemed*.
11	his hand To him *it seemed* so that he was	. . . . .↗.*it seemed*.
12	his hand.To him so that he was *He thought*	. . . :.*He thought*.
13	his hand To him so that he was	. . . .
14	his hand To him so that he was	. . . . .———————.
15	his hand To him so that he was	. . . .
16	his hand To him so that he was	. . . .———————.
17	his hand To him so that he was	. . . . .———————. . . .
18	his hand To him so that he was *He thought that*	.——. . . .*He thought that*.
19	his hand?To him so that he was	⌃⌃?∼∼∼∼. .
20	his hand To him so that he was *He felt that*	. . . .*He felt that*. .

Fig. 4: Rationalization of inadequate sentence-/thought-structure.

49

teachers of arts subjects to cope better with this latter demand than scientists or mathematicians, in view of their greater familiarity with extended personal writing, but in our experience this was not so. In general, it was the maths and science teachers who were more painstaking in their study of the script and more self-conscious about correcting what was in front of them, evidently appreciating they were breaking new ground. Ironically, it was a non-English specialist on the Arts side who slashed his way through the script in the shortest time of all and made the most strokes on the page — 66, on only 30 lines of writing!

The bar-chart we constructed (see Fig. 5) shows, in fact, a wild variation in the total numbers of strokes made on each script, yet even so there is not as big a gap between the maximum 66 and the next highest total as one might either have expected or hoped. There is an almost even progression from the lowest total (16) to the highest across the sample, with significant evening-out only at the 28 mark (a total achieved by four people), a level of correction which in itself averages out at virtually one stroke per line. Exactly two-thirds of the sample put 30 or more strokes on the page, a graphic reminder that wielding a red pen can be unthinkingly easy.

And what is a child to make of such a high level of correction? So much red ink trivializes the task of correcting, turning it more into a mistake-spotting drill than anything else. How might a child sort out what is of immediate and fundamental concern? The Bullock Report advocates greater caution in these terms:

> The teacher's first response to a piece of writing should be personal and positive. Only after responding to what has been said is it reasonable to turn attention to how ... Assessment is not in question; it is when it becomes an automatic and unvaried process that it loses its value for both teacher and pupil. When every piece of work receives detailed scrutiny on every occasion teachers are marking against the clock, and this is a further pressure towards confining the corrections to surface points.

In discussing 'surface points', we have a further telling example to offer. The sentence beginning in line 6 of the script (according to the writer's punctuation) ends with 'the boy sold it for 10$'. Those closing figures attracted much attention

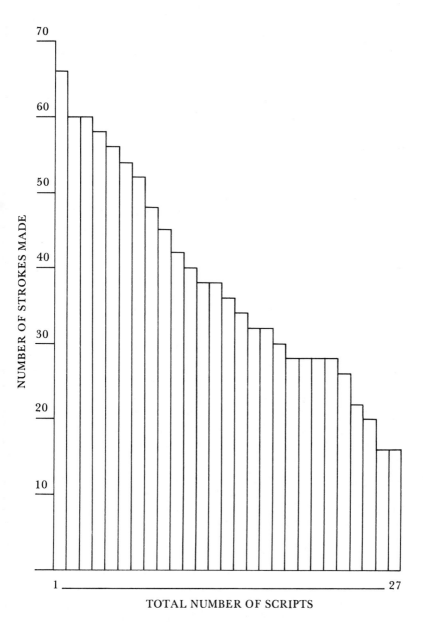

Fig. 5: Distribution of strokes made on scripts across the sample.

— so much so, in fact, that although the mistake in this instance is a relatively minor one, we found eleven alternative corrections across the sample. (See Fig. 6 below.)

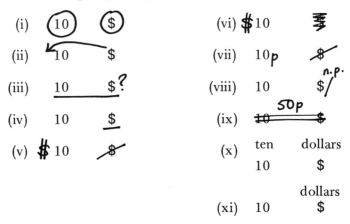

Fig. 6: Resolution of nonconformity to standard practice.

Two — items (x) and (xi) — reflect the purist view that small numbers in compositions should be written in words, not figures. A further three — items (i), (iii) and (iv) — could also be interpreted as reinforcing this idea, although they do not state it directly. Items (ii), (v) and (vi) show acceptance of the figures, but indicate that the dollar sign should precede '10'. This leaves items (vii), (viii) and (ix); in which cases cultural considerations appear to prompt the corrections, since British currency symbols are substituted for the American. Other figures used in the script were queried to nowhere near the same extent — '20' in the title, '2' in line 13, and '4' in line 14 receiving 4, 7 and 7 corrections respectively — thus supporting the inference that the 'trigger' was indeed the dollar sign itself. Bullock reminds us that:

> ... the most important step the teacher can take is to improve the pupil's confidence in his own capacity. Repeated failure reinforces a poor self-image, and the correction of written work can make matters worse unless its purposes are carefully worked out.

It would be undeniably disturbing to find that arbitrary cultural judgments such as we have just described were commonplace in the shaping of our pupils' self-images.

Several teachers awarded the composition marks out of 10, although this had not been specifically requested, with 4 the lowest and 7 the highest; while others gave grades that ranged from D up to B. This lack of agreement on the basic merit of the writing, already suggested by the widely differing total numbers of strokes on each script, was further reflected in comments appended by six of the teachers. Four, if terse, were basically encouraging — always accepting that 'See me!' is ambiguous. The remaining two, contrasting strikingly in tone and emphasis, read as follows:

(a) A very careless piece of work, you must think clearly before you write and try to organize your thoughts in a more. clearly orderly manner. Always read through your work. to iron out silly mistakes. Correct your spelling mistakes.

(b) What colour was the creature? What happened about the cage when the animal grew so fast?

In view of the reservations expressed in Chapter 2 about the effect of comments on a pupil's written performance, it may be worth noting here that the author of the second comment — a good response from engaged reader to writer, opening a potentially useful dialogue — saw herself as a generally poor corrector of her own pupils' day-to-day work. This emerged from discussing with her our interim findings, which were published and circulated locally in pamphlet form. She claimed to have benefited enormously by her participation in the experiment, since it had brought home to her for the first time how mechanical and negative most correcting is. Using a lot of red ink herself as a modern linguist, she felt the only way to offset its negativity was to follow up points individually with pupils in subsequent lessons.

This investigation provides evidence to support Bullock's contention that whilst non-English specialists may be competent language *users*, they are not automatically capable language *teachers*. In relation to our aim of exploring hierarchies of mistakes, we noted that the same mistakes were selected for attention in much the same order of priority by virtually everyone. However, the means (principally symbolic) by which corrections were indicated or effected differed considerably from one person to another and to this extent the limiting choice of test script enabled significant variations in practice to be identified.

Our single test script contained an interesting, yet manageable, range of fairly typical mistakes. Nevertheless, anyone mounting a similar enquiry might ideally use three examples of the same pupil's work rather than one. In addition to the 'imaginative/narrative' type of writing such as we used, specimens of, say, 'descriptive' and 'factual' writing might also be included. Although this would entail a more complicated analysis of results, it would offset the objection that straightforward stories are *usually* outside the experience of non-English specialists, and delineate more sharply the *range* of written work any given sample of teachers appeared capable of handling.

At the outset of the experiment we had intended to draw out a set of 'universal' correcting symbols from the completed scripts, to provide the nucleus of some form of standardized scheme, but given the actual diversity of notation, this proved impossible. Nevertheless, we persisted for a while in assuming that a small number of symbols to indicate pupil-error in the use of language could be extracted from the full range commonly used by English specialists, and that these could then be used in the same way by *all* teachers across the curriculum. The investigation exposed the flaw in this argument, for in terms of correcting and marking practices, the English specialist is *atypical* of teachers as a whole: certainly few other subject specialists seem to correct pupils' work in such fine detail except for teachers of modern languages. Conversely, there appears to be more in common between writing in subjects like history, geography and science, than between writing in any or all of those subjects and writing in English. Hence we concur with Nancy Martin (1977b) in her opinion that allowing oneself to be unduly preoccupied with devising standardized schemes for correcting and marking is to become 'remote from the major issue of the active role that language could play in learning'. Any solution to the conflict inevitably generated when pupils encounter variable standards of correction across the curriculum does not, therefore, conveniently lie embedded somewhere amidst the intricacies and pitfalls of standardization. Instead, it must somehow be rooted in the acceptance by teachers of a more sensitive and positive valuation of the uses of written language.

A second enquiry was conducted in association with the staff of an 8–12 middle school. The administrative circumstances in this instance were quite different. The headmaster selected the test script himself from writing produced by an eleven-year-old boy for science (Test Script 2: *Making a Microbalance* p.56) and distributed copies to all thirteen members of his staff to be corrected *within two minutes* in the course of a regular staff meeting. Thus there are elements of compulsion and surprise which will have had their effect upon these teachers.

Because the test script draws on material from a subject other than English and exhibits most of the features associated with *transactional* writing (whereas *20 million miles to Earth* would be classified as *poetic* writing), the analysis of this second set of results gives additional insights into the factors determining the relationship between writing, correcting and marking.

With the time-limit strictly enforced, several of the teachers felt compelled to append explanatory or self-justifying remarks to their completed scripts and these alone point to the mild degree of panic the exercise induced. Taken as a whole, they illustrate an appreciable diversity of outlook on the given task:

(a) I marked this as an English exercise presupposing that the pupil had knowledge/understanding of such terms as *measurement* and *piece*. Therefore marked incorrect words as sp.

(b) I marked this as an English teacher marking a science script. I would want to know who wrote it in order to be really helpful in my marking to the child who wrote it.

(c) This is marked as a piece of English. My marking would vary according to age and ability of child.

(d) Marked as an English exercise. I also know the child who wrote it.

(e) It would be more helpful to know the child to be able to mark it fairly to him.

(f) I have marked this as a science teacher marking a piece of science work.

(g) This has been marked as a piece of science work and not as an English composition.

(h) Not enough time.

Making a microbalance

First of all we got the weight of these
things to two sheets of paper weighs
44 gm 1 sheet weighs 4.4 80 big
squares weigh 55 mg   Then we
got the things needy we got two
straws, a piece of folded paper
a pin a screw a lolli-stick scale
a rubber band and a wooden block.
we then put the pin into the straw and
then fixed the two straws together
we put a scoop in the end of the straw
We then stuck the lolli lolli-stick to a
peice of wood with an elastic band. We
then put the screw into the end of the
straw and fixed the straw onto the
cradle. we then put the lolli stick
next to the end of the straw and
done some meaurments.

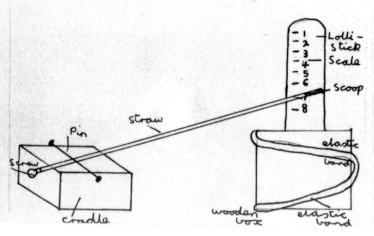

The ideal of fairness to the child-writer, mentioned more than once here, clearly distinguishes the middle-school class teacher's outlook from that of a secondary specialist. The distinction drawn between English and science, however, is less straightforward to explain. Why regard the test script as 'an English exercise' when it plainly isn't one? Presumably, the teachers meant that they wouldn't normally have marked a scientific piece like this, but would mark English in this way. Reaching any firmer conclusion is complicated by the fact that both the teachers admitting to a science bias correct many of the same technical *language* mistakes highlighted by their colleagues, so that although they perceive their approach to the script as being different, there is little visible evidence to that effect.

If any generalization can be made about the performance of these middle school, primary-trained, teachers, it is that there is a tendency to fall back on the stereotyped pattern of correction traditionally favoured by English specialists. Response to Martin's effort at a *personal* level is non-existent. Remarks addressed to him are brief, and likely to be construed as critical: 'what were the results?' for example, is more demanding than questioning when seen in context, yet the same end could be achieved by a simplified question like 'after you'd done this experiment, what had you discovered?' One teacher advises against the repetition of 'then', the only direct comment from anyone on the *style* of the piece. This apart, there are no attempts to influence the presentation of Martin's next science write-up; yet more guidance in this direction would seem to be crucial from a learning point of view.

Of course, the time-factor presents itself as a convenient excuse to explain some of these shortcomings. It assumes undue significance when a rigid limit is laid down: in practice, two minutes may well be the maximum amount of time spent by most teachers on the correcting and marking of one individual piece of writing. (Although examination marking is specifically outside the scope of this book, it is relevant here to remember that most experienced O Level English Language markers aim to mark 12—15 scripts an hour — an average of less than 5 minutes per candidate. The concern of the middle school teachers to avoid injustice pales into insignificance by comparison.) In addition, we have already seen that some of the teachers were wary of misjudging the effort of a child not known to them personally; but this point merely substantiates one made earlier about the strong influence of interpersonal factors and other hidden variables on teachers' correcting strategies (see Chapter 1, p.14).

Since ten of the thirteen teachers corrected every punctuation mistake and omission, we may conclude that a majority of the sample expected Martin to be capable of writing accurate standard English. (It could be fairly argued that inserting the missing commas in the first seven lines of text goes further towards satisfying the teacher who does that, than towards informing or educating the pupil who left them out in the first place.) Yet since the writing purports to be 'scientific', it would not be unreasonable to expect that *any* teacher's response to it might include some active encouragement of the use of the register appropriate to science. In fact, this is largely absent from the completed scripts.

No one queries the vague opening sentence ('First of all we got the weight of these things') nor the confusing way in which the subsequent record of weights obtained is totally unrelated in the account of the experiment to the ultimate calibration of the microbalance. No one suggests Martin might do better to draw up a table of known weights rather than list them, even though the ability to tabulate figures is a necessary complement to mature scientific writing. Whilst eleven teachers correct the verb form in the last line ('done some mesurments'), only three — two working from an English standpoint, and one as a scientist — offer 'took' in preference to 'did', and none of them proposes the better alternative 'made'.

The way in which the first half of the script attracts most of the teachers' attention amply illustrates the general point made in Chapter 1 about the need for correcting to be seen as a subsidiary function of thorough reading and comprehension (see pp.8—9). In the brief time allotted, effective reading could have revealed the problems of understanding, thinly masked in the last five lines, whereas none of the teachers touched on these. Indeed, those who follow the example of their first colleague, and profess an interest in the script as 'a piece of science work' by querying the absence of any results, miss the boy's inadequate grasp of the *method* in this experiment, and drive him on to accept the *conclusions*; yet since nowhere does he offer reasons for the activities he describes, it may well be that Martin has missed the point of the experiment altogether. If this is the case, then he needs help.

In conclusion, it emerges from a detailed examination of the scripts completed by both groups of teachers discussed in this chapter that a high proportion of the corrections relate to minor technicalities; and we may surmise this is because they are easiest to correct. In terms of the individual progress of pupils, however, that writing should be appropriate to any given circumstance is surely a more crucial factor than technical accuracy. As we have seen, close correction of scripts with a wide range of faults by means of symbolic notation alone does little, positively or negatively, to reinforce stylistic criteria. A teaching method which fails so completely to achieve its aims is normally rejected by teachers. It's curious that marking on that basis alone continues to be accepted at its face value.

Note

1 Twenty-seven teachers from the total staff of approximately eighty corrected Test Script 1 (q.v.), and a wide range of academic disciplines is represented by this sample. The subjects they taught (always remembering that some taught more than one) are as follows: English, Drama, Maths, History, Geography, French, Physics, RE, Needlework, Home Economics, Music, Technical Crafts, Commerce & Typing, General Subjects (Remedial), Modern Studies (Social Studies for non-academic fourth- and fifth-year pupils) and PE (Boys & Girls).

4 Some patterns of pupil involvement

Often . . . pupils are exhorted to check their 'language'.
The checking of grammar, syntax, the tone and appropriateness of the language, is fraught with hazards for the
learner, especially if he has any reason for being uneasy
about what is appropriate in the particular context, or if
the piece of writing is one on which he is being judged or
tested. Tests of linguistic acceptability are apt to be so
closely associated with subjective judgments about social
acceptability that the young writer may learn to mistrust
his own language and, by trying to be correct, stifle half
of what he wanted to say.

James Britton *et al* (1975)

Although most classroom teachers would claim to have used
pupils as markers in a rudimentary fashion at one time or
another, few will have actively encouraged them to review and
criticize their peers' writings with a view to enabling *pupils
themselves* to make comparative assessments of merit on a
regular basis. The idea presents itself as the logical extension of
a train of thought with a respectable pedigree which argues, in
the words of the Newbolt Report (1921), that the interchange
of pupils' own 'free and friendly criticisms' can do much to
improve the quality of writing in schools.

Investigating the possibilities for extending pupil-involvement
in the correcting process was admittedly remote from our
thoughts when we initiated our small-scale investigation. Nevertheless, having obtained an image in miniature of the impact that
years of noting teachers' corrections had made upon a small
group of seventeen-year-old students, we found ourselves at a
new point of departure. Certain sixth-formers had already
become peripherally involved in our original enquiry into
teachers' correcting strategies, studying *20 million miles to
Earth* as an exercise in practical criticism and one had alerted
us to the film source of the storyline. It is to this group of six

lower sixth A level students that we now turn to introduce some new ideas.

They received spare copies of Test Script 1 to study and correct, as we have said, the object being to help the students themselves appreciate the difficulties their own lapses of spelling, grammar and presentation created for readers of their essays. What emerges from an analysis of their completed scripts, however, goes beyond this particular aim and impinges upon our main area of concern.

As with the teachers, only the bare minimum of information about the writer was provided, since it was of interest to discover what assumptions would be made about his ability. Beyond this, however, there were three ways in which the test procedure varied from that followed for the main study: the students were free to spend as long as they wished on correcting the script, they were asked specifically both to award a suitable mark or grade and to write a comment and they were invited afterwards to discuss any problems they had encountered, with their completed scripts available for reference.

Being largely ignorant of standards of writing commonly achieved by younger pupils and free from any time-limit, the group understandably spent a long time simply reading through the script. When eventually they reached for their pens, they all tried to correct every mistake they had found, line by line. Although some words were crossed out, others underlined, and omissions indicated, the sixth-formers were much more inclined than the teachers were to write correct spellings or alternative phrasings above relevant errors or ambiguities. By this means, for example, the non-sentence beginning in line 10 was straightened out in at least two different ways:

(a) To him it seemed as if he was dreaming as he had seen nothing like that in his life before.
(b) It was as if he was dreaming as he had never seen anything like it in his life before.

It is interesting that these sixth-formers should have devoted more attention to resolving difficulties of this kind than to worrying unduly about spelling. Whilst it is true that five of the six did correct 'dinorsour', even in this instance one did so in the course of making a more fundamental alteration to poor phraseology, suggesting that 'a 4" animal/it was like a dinorsour'

61

(lines 14 & 15) might be better replaced by 'an animal, about four inches long resembling a dinasaur'. (The fact that yet another error in spelling 'dinosaur' was made by this student does not, in our view, invalidate his attempt at higher-level correction, and it may be excused by seeing him as deeply involved in reformulating the writer's meaning.)

There was complete agreement on changing 'lefted' to 'left', everyone crossing out the '-ed' to do so. Only one student thought fleetingly that 'lifted' might have been intended, and initially she crossed out the first 'e' and wrote 'i' above it, but she quickly crossed *that* out, restored 'e', and finally put a line through '-ed'. She went through this process quite unprompted by decisions reached by other members of the group and thus provided us with a clear illustration of the speed and mental agility correctors require if they are to do justice to the efforts of immature writers.

Only one mark (4/10) was given, the alternative of grades (ranging from C to B+) being generally preferred. Coupled with the critical tenor of the concluding comments, this may in part be an unconscious reflection of their own A level teachers' practices; but even so, it seems ironic that remarks composed by sixth-form students should be more scholarly in tone than those made by schoolmasters (and -mistresses) themselves. The self-assurance they embody is disarming:

(a) Good. Make your sentences shorter and try not to repeat phases. (The slip of the pen in 'phrases' is surely equivalent to that in 'dinasaur' above.)

(b) Quite a good attempt, but you must think more carefully before writing your ideas down as you have made some silly grammar mistakes. Do not be afraid to use a dictionary if you are not sure of spelling.

(c) You have a lively imagination, but you do not take enough care in constructing your sentences so that they make sense.

(d) A lot more care needs to be taken over the formation of sentences. Vocabulary requires more attention.

(e) Do not write in a series of short sentences and do not use the same conjunctions when combining the sentences.

(f) You have used wrong tenses in places. Some words are misplaced and you should check spelling, tenses, punctuation thoroughly before handing in.

In conversation afterwards, this group admitted to finding the set task very difficult, but nevertheless, by their own standards they performed it with some degree of competence. Obviously their inexperience prevented them from being more selective about the mistakes they chose to correct, but equally the sheer weight of correcting they undertook demonstrates how deeply they had absorbed the proscriptive norms applied to their own writing during their school career.

Having compared and contrasted teachers' and students' handling of identical material, we looked for other ways of examining more closely the assumptions about correctness that pupils might bring to bear upon their own writing. To this end, therefore, we fabricated a new test script, a one-paragraph story supposedly written by a semi-literate eleven- or twelve-year-old (Test Script 3: *On day I wented* p.64) and also devised a simple game in order to utilize it. A suitably cooperative, well-motivated secondary class was chosen, and divided into two halves. One half (Group A) were then given the script and asked to correct and mark it as if they were generally lenient and helpful teachers; whilst the other half (Group B) were to imagine they were teachers normally strict and unapproachable and correct their scripts accordingly. Beyond this guidance as to the roles they were to assume, both halves of the class were told to correct only what they felt necessary. In line with the first sixth-form experiment, every pupil was asked to award a mark or grade and to provide some comment. To establish some measure of comparison with our earlier work, a new lower sixth group was also invited to participate, but the main sample on this second occasion was a fourth-year set of twenty-eight pupils who had only been taught in that grouping for half-a-term.

(We purposely avoided choosing a class with a strongly developed sense of group-identity. We were also looking for pupils with a breadth of experience in terms of having been on the receiving end of a variety of teachers' correcting and marking practices. We conducted our research with this set shortly after it had been established at the start of a new school year, when the pupils in it, drawn from five equally new forms, had had little time to grow used either to each other, or to the methods of their new English teacher, who had taught very few of them before.)

On day I wented to the play ground and I seen a boy I knowed. Halo Jim I sed what you doing then Jim sed I am playing wit my football. I said can I play to no he wanted to play on his one. I was sad. He then sed alright Pete you be golkeper then you can play. We had a good game.

Looking at the set's performance in detail, the first significant point is that there is little to distinguish the scripts completed by one half from the other. If there is any noticeable trend towards an extreme, paradoxically it is that pupils in Group A corrected more mistakes than those in Group B. This suggests how difficult it is for pupils to take up a sympathetic, supportive stance as correctors of other pupils' efforts. Merely an invitation to do so is clearly not strong enough in itself to override personal prejudices or accumulated experience of how one's own efforts have been received in the past.

In fairness, however, it must be said that the deliberately pronounced artificiality of the script would set anyone an impossible task. Though considerably shorter than *20 million miles to Earth*, line for line it contains far more mistakes in unlikely collocation, while the prominence given to direct speech is an additional complication. Thus, whatever the stance assumed by a corrector, whether broadly supportive or regulative, we should expect to find an abnormally high proportion of corrections.

Leaving punctuation aside, there are four main categories into which the most obvious errors may be placed. These are the incorrect formation of the past tense of verbs — 'wented' (line 1), 'knowed' (line 3); confusion between the past *tense* and past *participle* — 'seen' (line 2); misspelling as a result of phonic miscues — 'sed' (lines 3, 4 & 8), 'one' (line 7) and misspelling as a result of visual confusion — 'On' (line 1), 'Halo' (line 3), 'wit' (line 5), 'to' (line 6), 'golkeper' (line 9). Very few pupils showed themselves able to differentiate between one type of mistake and another by singling out individual words or groups of words for special attention.

Nevertheless, there were two members of Group A who slanted their concluding remarks in this direction. The first has this to say: 'Good, but don't put ed on words and 'said' not sed like it sounds'. The second attempts a more comprehensive summing-up by itemizing three 'mistakes' in his first two sentences, but unhappily the first is a correction of a misreading and the third is prompted by his own ignorance of a simple rule:

Dont put ed on want, and watch out for said, not sed. When more than one thing it is too not to. Quite a good account but don't spell words as you hear them said. Well Done.

65

Although these pupils identified the frequently misleading relationship between the pronunciation and spelling of words, neither of them noticed or referred to 'said' in its correct form in line 6. Across the sample as a whole, members of both Group A and B corrected misspellings by rewriting them above the particular errors in the script, but only four of the twenty-eight (two from each group) suggested the writer needed to take further action himself. They did so in keeping with their allotted roles: the two members of Group A listed some corrections at the foot of the page and asked that they should be learned; the two from Group B, on the other hand, directed that the corrections already indicated should be completed in a traditionally formal manner. One required each wrong word to be rewritten, the other the entire piece!

These instances apart, nowhere was there any suggestion that the various spelling mistakes were anything but the result of carelessness. That is to say, the vast majority of the sample regarded them all as avoidable, given greater concentration on the part of the writer: possible misunderstanding or even ignorance of spelling patterns was not countenanced. Similarly, the poor punctuation was attributed to a lack of effort.

On most scripts the missing inverted commas were added, but as far as the direct-speech content of any story is concerned, providing the necessary punctuation solves only half the problem. Accomplished writers also know that for the sake of clarity special rules for layout must be applied. Yet no more than two pupils (both from Group A) laid stress on the need to open a new paragraph with every change of speaker, and neither could express the idea succinctly.

The first offers somewhat muddled advice: 'Remember to use new lines for different paragraphs when you talk about something else'. Study of his completed script, however, shows he has pointed out the need for a break to a new line only at the *second* change of speaker. The second appears more confident, and his recommendation ('Start new line when new speech starts'), though still not absolutely precise, is reinforced on his script by arrows running to the left of the page beneath lines 4, 5 and 6.

In terms of their final assessment of the piece, both groups conform almost too perfectly to their given types. Group B marked in the range from 3/10 to 5/10, or gave grades between E and C—; thus neatly abutting on to Group A's spread of marks from 5/10 up to 9/10 and grades from C+ to B—. Six pupils (two from A and four from B — in total less than a quarter of the set) took the game of being teacher to a more imaginative conclusion than their classmates by pretending their closing remarks had been framed with reference to a shared and continuing relationship with the writer. The resemblance in these few instances between the products of their role-play and typical responses from practising teachers is remarkable:

Group A — (a) Try and improve spelling, much better than last time, try and use speech marks.

          (b) Come and see me for correct spellings of words. Good try.

Group B — (a) This is a terrible piece of work. Care is needed in spelling and punctuation. See me!

          (b) Please see me about spelling. *Extra* care needed in both spelling and punctuation.

          (c) Your spelling and punctuation needs a lot more practise. If you paid more attention in class it would help. A lot of your mistakes are careless mistakes!

          (d) Your attitude to neatness, accuracy, and spelling needs a great deal more attention. Your presentation of this work is not satisfactory up to your age group standard. I advise you to pull up your socks and get to work. English is an important subject.

As to the sixth-formers who corrected the same script, they bear comparison with the fourth-years inasmuch as they too were members of a newly-established teaching group at the time of this experiment. Unfortunately, analysis of their performance can add little to our understanding of pupils' notions of correctness. Their role-play was over-enthusiastic to the extent that they spent most time trying to frame suitable concluding comments 'in character'. While it was interesting to see the supportive correctors amongst this group of eight earnestly addressing the writer at length, their persuasiveness was in reality almost wholly confined to *generalized* observations about Peter's poor spelling. Unlike their fourth-year counterparts, none of them isolated 'sed', nor did they list corrections to be learnt.

Furthermore, the advice they offered with regard to avoiding future difficulties with both spelling and presentation was sometimes only superficially helpful. In the following example, for instance, the first half of the third sentence does not relate to the two preceding sentences, whilst the second half relates imperfectly to another assumption held by the student in question. Thus intended simplification induces actual mystification:

> Try to sound out the word before you write it down. This will improve your spelling. Read it through before handing it in, put a full stop where you breathe. A good effort. Well Done.

Even so, this student was not alone in stating a naïve belief in the power of 'reading through' as a useful technique for eliminating errors; teachers themselves commonly give similar advice to senior pupils in the run-up to external examinations. 'Reading through', however, can only be of value to a pupil once he or she has been trained to do it with a specific object in mind: it is, in other words, a sophisticated process that writers acquire when they are conscious of what they are trying to achieve and so it is something that needs nurturing and not something to be proffered lightly as a cure-all. Seen from this standpoint, those students assigned supportive roles failed to draw any significant moral from the exercise — unlike one of the regulative group who warned the writer to 'think more about the quality of what you write'.

In both classes, no assessment was made of the story's content in its own right and no invitation to reappraise its likely impact on a specified reader was extended to the writer. Although Test Script 3 is undeniably weak and indeed bogus as a piece of storytelling, why did nobody say so? The answer may, of course, lie in the constraints imposed by the nature of the given task itself. After all, the classes were instructed to *correct* the script rather than *read* it, which takes us back to our earlier point about differences in expectations between teachers and pupils (see pp.3–4 above). Or perhaps weaknesses in style are not so readily apparent to younger minds — an unlikely explanation here, in view of the above-average ability and academic orientation of the participants.

A final possibility may be that teachers' handling of their own written work has conditioned these pupils to judge competence simply in terms of technical accuracy, so that when they assumed teachers' roles themselves, they automatically applied that criterion to the exclusion of all others.

We next tackled the question of how to make the correcting of scripts easier and more worthwhile, to see if we could find a way of helping pupils to criticize each other's writing helpfully. The simplified scheme we eventually devised employs only three basic symbols (the line, asterisk, and omission sign), but its object is to convey *positive* information, based on thorough reading, from corrector to writer. By definition, therefore, it is *not* a diluted form of proof-reading, which not only employs a large number of symbols with very precise applications but also requires *skimming* on the part of the proof-reader and no real attention to the meaning of the text.

It departs from standard practice in that a line is drawn under phrases or sentences considered to be good, whilst mediocre or incomprehensible passages are left unmarked; the idea behind this being that the writer should receive a strong and immediate impression of his overall level of achievement. The use of the asterisk deliberately imitates the adult use of the footnote, as reinforcement of a specific reading skill: it denotes a misspelling, and is repeated at the foot of the page together with the corrected version of the word. If more than one is found necessary on any given page, then they are numbered sequentially, e.g. $*^1$, $*^2$. The omission sign, an inverted V in its commonest form, appears to be as universal as the tick or cross, (hence its inclusion in the scheme) and can be as useful for indicating missing punctuation as it obviously is for showing up missing words.

To date, we have experimented with this system on a strictly limited basis, yet even so, not only have we demonstrated that children can respond to it readily, but also that they are quite capable of operating it effectively for themselves. The initial teacher-directed stage of our work in this field was undertaken with a class of average-ability twelve-year-olds in a secondary school, with the sole aim of establishing the extent of the scheme's practicability. As part of their normal English programme, the pupils were offered a choice of titles on which to write a composition, to fill no more than one side of A4 file paper. They were allowed one lesson to begin the task, then their papers were collected in and corrected accordingly.

Equally important, however, is the fact that each piece of work also received an interim comment, usually referring to stylistic features and potential for further development of ideas, *but no mark or grade*. In the next English lesson the work was returned and every pupil was recommended to study carefully corrections and comments alike before proceeding to complete the composition.

Processing the writing of some thirty children in this manner took between two and three hours, the trial run naturally taking longer than a comparable amount of work under normal everyday circumstances. Nevertheless, the pupils' enthusiastic response to a correcting scheme they could readily interpret was complemented by their spontaneous discussion of each other's efforts. As they went on to finish their work, modification of their written performance in the light of the guidance offered became apparent.

Such an outcome prompted the need for further experimentation, to see whether immature writers below secondary level could benefit from the scheme's introduction or, furthermore, apply it themselves to rough drafts *independently of a teacher*. To this end, therefore, we sought the cooperation of an all-age class of seven- to eleven-year-olds in a small rural primary school. Again, the writing to be the focus of attention represented one aspect of the regular pattern of classwork, although it took the form of a short poem rather than a full-length composition and had been produced as an adjunct to seasonal art work depicting the Christmas story. This time, however, having explained the correcting scheme to the children, the class teacher delegated the responsibility for correction and criticism to them.

From the results obtained, two important conclusions may be drawn: that pupils need not be prevented from correctly *identifying* mistakes in their peers' writing by their own incomplete knowledge of precise spellings and that pupils would seem best able to make formal judgments on the *quality* of writing in the absence of pressure towards awarding marks or grades. (Both these conclusions, but especially the latter, represent significant departures from our secondary school findings, of course.) These points notwithstanding, the systematic and profitable involvement of young children, including some very inexperienced writers, in an essentially critical exercise must surely be regarded as the principal achievement of this particular trial lesson and should compel us, in anticipation of the final Chapter, to revise our ideas of how competence in the written mode should be both fostered and measured.

70

5 The accommodation of rehearsal: implications for policy and practice

> ... when he has written a rough draft of his Essay, let him read it over very carefully, that he may make such corrections as occur to him before putting it into its final shape.
>
> James Currie (1884)

> The teacher's job is not to correct mistakes the pupil has already made, but to help him not to make that mistake next time.
>
> Mike Torbe (1977)

The fundamental premise around which this study has been constructed is that amidst the continuing debate on approaches to the assessment of language performance, one stark fact has been persistently overlooked — namely, that we in the teaching profession do not possess a well-articulated *theory of correctness* and certainly not one that might at present be conveniently extended across the curriculum.

It transpires that even today, many teachers still tend to judge pupils' writing abilities largely by reference to an intuitive model, perhaps more aptly described by Peter Doughty *et al* (1972) as a *folk linguistic*, a collection of unquestioned assumptions about the nature and function of language. Unhappily, the cumulative effect of prolonged application of such folk-linguistic norms to relevant areas of the curriculum would seem to be to institutionalize arbitrariness, if not chaos. Nor is there scope within the folk-linguistic ambit to accommodate contemporary theories of language and learning. As Pat D'Arcy (1977) puts it, 'writing which is disorganized, which makes mistakes and shows confusions of thought, tends still to be regarded by the teacher *evaluatively*'; whereas current research argues for 'a more positive *valuing* of mistakes as an inevitable and necessary part of learning anything'.

Mistakes, in fact, must assume a new importance in their own right if they are to be accepted as indicators of the stage of

71

rehearsal a writer has attained. The psychological factors governing the writing process itself are as yet imperfectly understood, but it is useful to think of a writer as rehearsing optimal intentions with each successive draft, striving each time to achieve a more satisfying compromise between the mesh of ideas in one's head and the words appearing on the page. But this balance which the writer seeks also requires other, more subtle adjustments, which James Britton (1975) believes may be condensed into two broad principles as follows:

> There is the need to get it right in terms of the facts of the case and what is generally known or accepted; these may of course be challenged or rejected but cannot normally be ignored. There is also the need to get it right with the self, the need to arrive at the point where one has the satisfaction of presenting what is to be presented in the way one thinks it should be done.

For the immature writer (and the pupil in school in particular), the greatest need for help exists at the preliminary level, that of the formulation of meaning, rather than at the later stage of presentation — and especially in academic subjects with both a high factual and theoretical content like history, geography, and the sciences. Yet, as we have seen, such assistance is not readily forthcoming.

If we look for a moment at the broad picture emerging from our own investigation, we can clearly see that the trend towards the negative evaluation of children's writing is indeed as pronounced as Pat D'Arcy asserts; for although evaluative judgments (which, put crudely, reflect the merit of written work in terms such as 'poor', 'fair' and 'good') may have been legitimized through their continuing acceptance by pupils, parents and teachers, this is not to say that in reality they mean a great deal. Furthermore, it is wrong to assume that judgments which are accompanied by marks or grades are in any true sense more useful or objective than those that are not, since it is possible to *grade* children's writing without any actual empathy with the child-writer and what he or she is trying to do.

The most crucial factor in determining the effectiveness of any teacher's correcting strategy is undeniably the impact it has upon the pupils. If the meaning conveyed to a child by corrections is nil, or, even given understanding, if the response a child can make to corrections is nil, then it is *the teacher's approach* that needs revising. But how is this to be done when the persistence of evaluative judgments continues to lay powerful constraints upon both perpetrator and recipient of corrections?

For instance, it may often *appear* that the same deficiencies or virtues in a pupil's writing have been discovered by a number of different subject teachers, as could conceivably be the case in the upper years of middle school or at any level in secondary school — whereas *in fact*, as we should be aware, responses to work across the curriculum are determined by wholly variable and often conflicting criteria. 'Good' in science is *not* equivalent to 'good' in geography, nor to 'good' in English and this is precisely why evaluative terminology causes problems, particularly with regard to monitoring pupil achievement. Even when an identical description of the quality of work done has been offered by two or more teachers, be it 'good' or 'poor', we cannot properly make the assumption that it denotes any comparability of performance whatsoever. Yet it remains expedient for many teachers, pupils and parents alike to draw that very inference.

Our examination of Michael's secondary school writing in Chapter 2 showed clearly the differences in attitude, or stance, adopted by a variety of subject specialists towards his work. What is more, our limited sampling of teachers' correcting strategies (as reported in Chapter 3) revealed wide discrepancies of practice *at the level of the individual word* and with this documentation to hand, we are more strongly in a position to speculate as to why such variations arise.

They are already accounted for in part by the range of academic contexts in which writing occurs in school: different disciplines generate different linguistic expectations, for the teacher as much as for the pupil. Asked, for instance, to identify a 'typical' scientific or historical text, most of us could predict quite accurately the grammatical and stylistic features we should expect writing for these subjects to display. Where difficulties do occur, however, is in the realm of teacher/reader response — how far, in other words, the significance of the actual language chosen is overshadowed by the demand for appropriacy of register and accuracy of content — and here, we confront the varying degrees of skill with which teachers read effectively and in turn the varying degrees of open-mindness and linguistic awareness teachers display in their scrutiny of pupils' work.

Some inflexibility in this direction logically derives from the extent to which teachers see themselves as guardians of a well-defined body of knowledge. If we revert to Michael's work again for a moment, we can see plainly that his French teacher possessed just such a highly developed sense of correctness from an academic standpoint. Wherever there is an extreme division of outlook between teacher and pupil, there seems little prospect of opening up the situation in order to ease the learning burden for the child. Under these circumstances, the principal focus of attention is knowledge itself, rather than the response to it. Teachers who see their main role as disseminators of knowledge in their chosen specialism are disposed to see it as their responsibility alone to monitor the pupils' acquisition of that knowledge most scrupulously.

If we seek further to assess teachers' commitment to the ideal of 'knowledge' over the curriculum as a whole, we may well arrive at a conceptual model of teacher-behaviour closely resembling the 'Transmission/Interpretation' dichotomy propounded by Douglas Barnes (1976) in which the 'transmission teacher' sees the job of teaching as being to transmit knowledge and then testing to see if the pupils have received it; while the 'interpretation teacher' feels that the pupils' ability to re-interpret knowledge is crucial to learning, and sees that as depending on a productive dialogue between the pupil and the teacher. 'Transmission' is not associated with one set of subjects and 'interpretation' with another, since such a model can discriminate only between individual teachers' perceptions of role and the concomitant effects on performance. The model, by Barnes's own definition, accounts largely for the higher intellectual dimension of a teacher's activities, rather than considering the impact of organizational constraints upon teaching styles. How any teacher mediates between subject and pupils is admittedly determined in large part by his or her personal conception of what properly constitutes 'knowledge' and 'learning', but it is also considerably affected by pressures from the school organization, not least from the implications of time-tabling.

Tension generated by time-tabling for the individual teacher derives from three inter-related sources: the juxtaposition of classes on any given day; the differential weighting given to classes in terms of their total period allocation; and the availability and spread of non-teaching periods. Naturally the full force of any combination of these factors is more likely to be felt by secondary specialists than by primary-class teachers. Yet if we now consider the reception of children's written work in this light, we may be surprised to find that the amount of free time a teacher is allowed probably has *least* to do with the quality of criticism and correction he or she can offer. This is because the habitual effect of the first two factors taken together is to compel private decisions, by each individual member of a school staff, about the order of his or her teaching priorities and the function of correcting depends on whose work is being marked and where in that order of priorities the work stands. If this explanation correctly pinpoints important constraints on teachers, and if it therefore reflects the thinking underlying much current practice in schools today, then by implication it is damning, especially because of its effects upon the way teachers monitor and evaluate their pupils' growth of competence in writing.

Looked at most simply, a teacher's decision to devote more attention to some classes than others, for whatever reason, will lead almost inescapably to more cursory reading and less explicit correction of written work from children in those classes which the teacher has chosen to rate as a low-priority. If priority work is to be processed to the teacher's own satisfaction, the consideration that can be given to the rest must necessarily be scant. In effect, since circumstances will preclude the framing of all but the tersest of comments, there is a breakdown of correcting and marking as a means of communication between teacher and low-priority pupil — and the lower the priority any given pupil has in a teacher's overall schema, the more abstract the nature of the corrections to the written work is likely to be and the greater the reliance the teacher is likely to place on convenient, but unexplained symbolic notation rather than words and phrases.

If our identification of the root cause of teachers' ineffectual reception of written work at *some* levels of operation is correct, then the progress of low priority pupils must necessarily become our immediate concern. It should, nevertheless, be understood that this is not simply a resurrection of issues from the long-standing debate on equality of educational opportunity: the iniquities of poor practice in relation to the correction and criticism of writing may be felt as much by the bright child as by the less able. Indeed, to recall the example offered in Chapter 1 of the low priority a first-year intake class might receive by comparison with a fifth-year examination group, this makes clear the fuller implications of the situation we have outlined. There is already documentary evidence in the work of Patrick Creber (1972) of 'a conditioning process designed to render pupils quiescent' in their first year at secondary school to lend independent support to our own point of view.

The inference may therefore be drawn that superficial correction is often symptomatic of a poorly-developed teacher-pupil relationship. Yet it can also reflect a teacher's narrow conception of what constitutes an appropriate response to the pupils' writing. The increasing predominance of the role of the teacher-as-examiner which children encounter as they move up through the secondary school and which means they grow more and more disposed to write 'with the expectation of assessment rather than response', has already been well documented by James Britton *et al* (1975), not only with reference to age but also to specific subjects. (Whilst 40 per cent of scripts from first-years in a national sample submitted to the Writing Research Unit were judged to be directed towards the teacher-as-examiner, the corresponding figure for fifth-years was 52 per cent. Of the writing in the sample, 69 per cent drawn from history, 81 per cent from geography, and 87 per cent from science was considered to be similarly orientated.) Hence Nancy Martin *et al* (1976) justifiably drew the conclusion that many children must view writing more as a *testing* than a *learning* task:

> . . . that so much of secondary school writing appears to be concerned with assessment is worrying because it suggests that the more important function of writing – its potential contribution to the mental, emotional and social development of the writer – is being neglected.

The way work is marked, which is generated by this focus or assessment, has a direct effect upon the kinds of writing that pupils actually produce. In this connection, transactional writing – widely used 'to record facts, exchange opinions, explain and explore ideas, construct theories . . . ' – has again been shown to predominate both with age and in certain subjects. (Of first-year writing in the Writing Research Unit's sample,

54 per cent was classified as transactional, rising to 62 per cent in the fifth year; this form was found in 88 per cent of the writing for history and geography, and in 92 per cent of the writing for science.) From this, it emerges that children are not being sufficiently encouraged to use writing to explore new ideas *in depth,* since the preponderance of transactional writing is taken to indicate that pupils largely use a received adult model for written work which they have not been given the opportunity to work towards on their own terms first. Thus we may expect that:

> ... what pleases the teacher, what he considers to be the appropriate language of his subject and the appropriate way of using it, may not be helpful — indeed may actually impede the understanding of his pupils.[1]

For significant change to take place, however, there must be the will within a school not only for radical action by the individual teacher, but also by departments and ultimately the whole school. New approaches to written work cannot be effected without revising ideas of classroom management and control, hence the deliberate inclusion of 'policy' in the heading for this Chapter. If we are to redress the balance against the undervaluing of what Mike Torbe (1978) has succinctly described as *first-draft learning,* then what is required, as suggested earlier, is the development of a more comprehensive theory of correctness — which by definition cannot be undertaken in isolation.

The overall guiding principle of such a revitalized theory must be *the accommodation of rehearsal*; that is, the willing acceptance, interpretation and exposition of mistakes that either denote a lack of clear thinking or understanding on the part of the writer, or create difficulties for the reader. Two important aspects of the theory in operation must consequently be *evidence of comprehension* and *negotiation of acceptability*. Both these concepts offer the basis for correcting strategies qualitatively different in orientation from those we discovered in common use.

Were it not signally lacking in the samples of correcting we assembled, *evidence of comprehension* would otherwise seem too obvious perhaps for inclusion here. Yet it should also be remembered that pupils feel its absence keenly, if not resentfully. The definition of comprehension cited earlier (on p. 9) is still the one by which we mean to proceed, since it lays the requisite stress upon a reader *actively* engaging with the meaning writers are attempting to convey by their choice of words. (As we have already seen, so much in the way of traditional correcting and marking is superficial, in that it indicates that the teacher/reader is attending only to surface details.) Nevertheless, actually providing evidence of such engagement is more difficult than some teachers might imagine. It requires more than the ubiquitous tick, so it must impinge upon teaching priorities to the extent that they also have to be revised.

As to the precise form which this evidence of engagement will take, it has to be governed by careful consideration of a pupil's ability and motivation to interpret and respond to it. This is one direction in which traditional procedures seem most often at fault, as amply illustrated by the example of Michael's French teacher. Yet whilst respect for individual differences between pupils should be shown, their existing competence at handling language should not be underestimated. The overview we have of Michael's writing reveals the partial nature of the grasp which each of his teachers, working largely in isolation, had of his comparative strengths and weaknesses; whereas it also tells us a great deal about his overall rate of progress towards eventual fluency in a variety of registers. After all, in respect of the sheer total of words, syntactic and grammatical structures produced, he got far more right than he ever did wrong; an obvious point, maybe, but one all too easily overlooked.

For criticism to be potentially effective, therefore, it must initially refer to specific aspects of what has been written, and apply only to the writer as an individual. Too often we seem able to make only generalized statements, which carry a seemingly universalized force, although in reality it is well understood that what is acceptable in the register of one subject is not necessarily so in another. (How far, for example, is a comment like 'Be careful your sentences do not become too similar in their construction' — see Chapter 2, p.25 — a *general* rule?)

A further precept to be considered is that in general 'open' responses to writing received seem preferable to 'closed' ones, even if the work itself has been produced and accepted as the conclusion to a specific line of enquiry or study. In both samples of teacher-corrected scripts we found repeated examples of 'closed' comments or questions, requiring little or no response in turn from the pupils themselves and often expressed in imprecise evaluative phraseology, but hardly any that could be called 'open'. One from the secondary sample is quoted as example (b) on p.53. By contrast, no teacher from the middle school sample offered anything comparable, although the potential for 'open' responses to factual writing is ably shown by Michael's second-year general science teacher, quoted on pp.29—34. Failure to lead children on to reflect upon what they have already written (as distinct from what they might move on to next) through selective use of stimulating, personal questions or observations represents an opportunity sadly wasted, for both teacher and learner. A teacher should always be able to say *something* about *any* piece of children's writing he or she is offered, *on the basis of textual evidence alone*; if he or she fights shy of direct comment, then professional responsibility is abdicated. He or she cannot assume the critic's authority at one time in the classroom by, say, interpreting information and opinions presented in textbooks and plead ignorance at another.

However, whether the evidence that the pupil's writing has been understood is written or spoken (and the spoken word may very often be preferable, better heeded for being less distancing), it need not — and indeed cannot — always emanate from the teacher. The issue of the peer-group standing as a wider audience for writing was raised in Chapter 4, the imitative formality of senior secondary pupils being contrasted with the striking adaptability of much younger children under differing trial conditions. Involving the pupils not only in the writing itself but also in the study of the effectiveness of writing offers itself as a deliberate means to an end which the teacher is unlikely to achieve unaided; the possibility does exist that an adult may be too *sophisticated* a reader to be of constructive assistance to an immature writer. As John Pearce (1972) sees it, 'our readiness to be put off by a piece of written language is often a reflection not so much of the language used, as of our own knowledge and experience'. Children themselves are less overloaded with such preconceptions, especially of a linguistic kind and can therefore often be more receptive than adults to ideas finding expression only at the level of *hesitant command.*

Hesitant command has been defined by Peter Doughty *et al* (1972) as the penultimate stage in the growth of competence in both speech and writing and for writing represents that stage of first-draft learning or rehearsal to which we have referred above. In time, it should lead to the final stage of *fluent command*, yet paradoxically teachers rarely oversee this transition:

> ... the kind of writing most often required of pupils, rational exposition and argument, is precisely the kind of writing that is most dependent upon a careful and often extended process of *Hesitant command* before a text can be produced which an experienced reader would accept as fluent. The corollary of this is that most teachers cannot, therefore, expect to see very often a text which is truly fluent, because the writer is seldom allowed the time required, or given the motivation, for raising a hesitant version to a fluent version.

That discussion between pupils about written work should be incorporated into what can readily be justified as already overfull teaching programmes will doubtless be asking too much of many subject specialists, but regular lessons of reading and study across the curriculum, in which the prime focus of attention is on the pupils' writing itself, appear a necessary and timely counterbalance to the trends outlined earlier. More specifically, such lessons would represent a positive advance insofar as they relieved the teacher of the burden of posing as the sole arbiter of acceptability all the time, which at present contrives to make so much in the way of correcting and marking so tedious. Furthermore, they would require the teacher to consider more carefully and make more explicit the criteria by which the effectiveness of a piece of writing may be judged, since he or she would have to initiate and supervise these lessons in an openly advisory capacity.

As an indicator, at least, of what can be achieved at the outset in this direction, we can here refer to the experience of a second-year class in a secondary school, in whose English lessons study and discussion of writing amongst pupils features regularly. After only one term they reached the point of being able to make genuinely critical judgments, and were given instructions as follows:

1 Give your opinion of the story you've just read.
2 Award it the grade you feel it deserves (from A—E) and explain why you've chosen that grade, if it isn't apparent

from your first comment. (Whilst this step blatantly contradicts an important conclusion drawn at the end of Chapter 4, in the school concerned, grading is the universally accepted system of reward.)

3   Comment on any *weaknesses* in the piece of writing, as you see it.
4   Suggest ways in which the writer could avoid these difficulties in future.

The first two instructions were already quite familiar. The last two were new to the children and they provoked a wide-ranging response, and a useful classification of weaknesses for future reference eventually emerged from the lesson (see Fig. 7 below).

Weakness	No of pupils identifying fault
Handwriting	14
Poor ending	7
Paragraphing	6
General lack of interest or excitement	4
Spelling	3
Punctuation	3
Repeated crossings-out	3
Uneven quality of writing	3
Bad grammar	1
Story hard to follow	1
Story far-fetched	1
Story failing to live up to title	1
Misuse of capitals	1
Lack of description	1

Fig. 7: Peer-group identification of specific weaknesses in imaginative writing produced by twenty-seven twelve-year-olds.

This was, of course, the outcome of an analysis of imaginative writing, but even if factual accounts are to be examined, the basic principle involved remains the same and thus the individual teacher is freed to do more direct teaching of the uses of language. What we have to recognize, however, is that for this scheme to succeed, the *criteria* for the analysis of writing must be seen by the child to vary from subject to subject, so that in science, for instance, the inability of a second person to replicate the results of an experiment by following a pupil's original firsthand account of it has to be presented as a greater weakness than poor handwriting or misuse of capitals in the same piece of work. These differences have to be *consciously taught*. It is a false supposition that the English department will somehow always act as a 'language service unit' to the rest of the school and that pupils' presumed inadequacies in written self-expression across the curriculum may continually be referred back to their English teachers. It is neither in English lessons nor at the instigation of English specialists that pupils are ordinarily required to write in the registers of history, geography or physics. If there is a set of specialized terms which the science department expects pupils to understand and be able to use at a certain stage of learning, then it becomes primarily the science department's responsibility to devise a means of achieving this.

It can, in fact, be argued that a new impetus in respect of the place and function of writing is urgently needed in all academic subjects, not just in English itself, since it is in the most heavily loaded content areas of the curriculum that the interdependence of writing and learning assumes greatest significance. Even the correcting strategy *traditionally* associated with English specialists seems atypical of teachers as a whole, as noted in Chapter 3, and the teacher-as-grammarian role is demonstrably inadequate beyond very tightly-defined limits.

Turning now to the *negotiation of acceptability*, we confront the key concept underpinning any theory of correctness which is accommodating rather than proscriptive. It has to do with 'getting it right', that challenge implicit in the setting of any written task in school — finding the right words to establish the right meaning in the right context — yet admitting the possibility that there is more than one way to do it; it is in this light that first-draft learning may still come into its own. What is *aceptable* may not at first appear directly equivalent to what is correct, but it may be if what is written adequately conveys meaning relevant to the context in which it is intended to be read. The process of negotiation permits the writer, as much through exploratory talk as through preparing alternative drafts, to progressively modify performance in line with these contextual demands, namely to meet the needs of the reader who will be at the receiving end of a particular piece of writing.

If the constraint of being assessed against an undisclosed yet all-pervasive standard is lifted from pupils' shoulders, then the audience for writing need no longer be conceived as the teacher-as-examiner and writer and teacher together can determine what is to be 'correct' for this particular purpose. By agreeing to approach writing more as a cooperative endeavour, teacher and pupils (or pupils together) can thus utilize the full range of forms, other than the narrowly transactional, to explore the effective recording and transmission of new ideas. What is to be negotiated will be both what the writing is to include and exclude and also its surface and structural features — its layout, paragraphing, formality and so on — since ultimately they affect the clarity of communication; but this will be done systematically in anticipation of a final draft.

Negotiation means that the teacher has to be prepared to adjust to individual differences amongst the pupils and be willing to support a variety of approaches to writing in line with those differing needs, which the setting of the whole-class one-lesson assignment tends to mask. Donald Graves (1978) makes this last point in the course of postulating two identifiable types of child-writer, the *reactive* and the *reflective*, who approach the task of writing in very different ways. The reactive writer has to talk things over first, writes slowly and tends to compare sentence by sentence, while the reflective writer doesn't need to rehearse ideas first, writes quickly and tends to know what the whole piece will be about. Afterwards, the reactive writer puts the work away quickly, pleased it's finished, but the reflective will re-read it, tinker with the words and perhaps show it to others.

Negotiation also makes it possible to reflect on, and discuss with pupils, the appropriateness of paper, pens and pencils — the actual writing materials available to them. The standard exercise book, for instance, has several obvious disadvantages, the chief one being that it is essentially a 'closed' means of communication. The work it contains is relatively inaccessible and appears in an inconveniently random order; even the page-size often imposes implicit restrictions on the output of average or less able pupils. In many ways, a loose-leaf folder might be better. It can be properly indexed, single sheets or complete sub-sections may simply be added, or removed for photocopying or display and suitable illustrative material may easily be inserted. Nevertheless, some pupils may see security in the comparative permanence of a book, and classroom filing systems are notoriously unreliable unless skilfully managed.

As for writing implements, at various stages of completing a given task a writer may find pencil, felt-tip, ball-point or cartridge pen all of use. Children therefore need to explore the options each one opens in terms of ease of manipulation and quality of presentation. Even if this sounds more applicable to a first school than a secondary school, we suspect many older children cannot overcome handwriting and layout problems because they have missed this sort of experience. If adults can be stuck for thought for want of a favourite pen or the right paper, why not children?

As to the extent to which negotiation permits detailed monitoring and assessment of pupils' progress, this will be governed by the level of teacher-pupil interaction attained. However, since the object of teaching and encouraging writing over a period of time is to help children improve their writing, careful observation alone should provide a teacher with information which is more likely to help than interminable columns of marks and grades. Whilst the function of correcting can be absorbed into discussing and refining exploratory drafts, 'marking' will be reduced to one of a number of possible alternative responses to a finished piece of work. If publication is proposed (either within the classroom or for a wider readership, as the ultimate test of readability), then there may be a place for proof-reading along lines such as those suggested by Nancy Martin (1968). But since proof-reading appears historically to be the basis for conventional correcting strategies, it must be regarded as essentially negative outside its proper confines. Nor can it stand in place of fuller evidence of comprehension: the proof-reader attends to the degree of technical expertise a writer displays, not to the quality or the meaning of what is written.

Ensuring continual feedback from reader to writer is perhaps the most important element of response to be considered part of negotiation. When the writer wants to know if what is being written makes sense, then comments should apply only to the writer as an individual and to what he or she has actually written. When a writer later seeks confirmation of acceptability for the writing, then feedback has actively to help consolidate a stage of learning and hence should relate individual flaws or strengths to abstract principles of language in use and to the universalized functions of writing as well as to the specific response to *this* piece of writing.

At present, transfer from primary to secondary schooling gives particular cause for concern, because of the secondary school's narrowly functional orientation to the use of language. Pupils from good primary schools, where they have learned the variety of uses to which written language may be put and the forms it may take, suddenly find themselves at a disadvantage because many of the familiar options disappear in the secondary school. Some of them may suffer as they try to adjust, without help, to the new limited demands. Although external examinations ultimately require pupils to possess highly specialized transactional writing skills, schools should lay proper foundations for the eventual acquisition of this kind of writing by making sure that in the first years teaching methods are supportive and coordinated, as the Bullock Report recommended:

> In the secondary school there is the additional complexity that the pupil is now writing for a number of different teachers and with an increased range of constraints. There are the words he needs for his own purposes but also the words the subject teacher requires him to have, and the uncertainty can be sharply increased within a matter of weeks. This calls for a high degree of patience and co-operation on the part of the staff.

Our concluding chapter has necessarily laid more stress upon theoretical considerations than detailed revisions of practice in the knowledge that every school presents a different organizational context for the use of language by pupils and staff. This may be unfortunate, for as Patrick Creber (1978) has observed, 'in our culture and especially in school teaching "practical" is a term with strong overtones of approval, whereas the word "theoretical" evokes a largely negative or hostile response'. Change only begins with a reappraisal of the adequacy of the theory underlying established practice yet with the correction

85

and criticism of writing, such theory, where it can be expressed at all, is patently thin and tenuous.

In preparing this study for publication we have been conscious throughout of the deep-seated suspicion with which many teachers view reports of educational research, and we have therefore tried to keep it as simple and straightforward as possible. But this is not to deny (again in Patrick Creber's words) 'the extent to which teachers, *in their normal operations*, employ theoretical constructs'. Paradoxically, we have ourselves employed a standard (and thus suspect) academic medium as a vehicle for new thinking, but if by so doing we can persuade fellow teachers to look for ways in which their marking of children's written work can help their pupils to learn more effectively, then our efforts will not have been in vain.

Note

1 Quoted from Nancy Martin (1977a). Full details of the research undertaken by the Writing Research Unit, working under James Britton's direction at the London University Institute of Education, are contained in James Britton *et al* (1975); and the application of their findings is considered at length in Nancy Martin *et al* (1976) — the two works between them covering the research and developmental stages of the Schools Council Project Writing Across the Curriculum.

Bibliography

ATKINSON, Richard (1975) 'Marking as a Mechanism of Social Control'; *English in Education* Vol 9 No 1. Oxford University Press, for NATE

BARNES, Douglas (1969) *Language, the learner and the school* Penguin Education

BARNES, Douglas (1971) 'Classroom Contexts for Language and Learning'; *Educational Review* Vol 23 No 3. Birmingham University School of Education

BARNES, Douglas (1976) *From Communication to Curriculum* Penguin Education

BOARD OF EDUCATION (1914) *Handbook of Suggestions for the Consideration of Teachers and others concerned in the work of Public Elementary Schools* HMSO

BOARD OF EDUCATION (1937) *Handbook of Suggestions for the Consideration of Teachers, etc. . . .* HMSO

BRIGGS, D. (1970) 'The Influence of Handwriting upon Assessment' *Educational Research* Vol 13 No 1

BRITTON, James *et al* (1975) *The Development of Writing Abilities (11—18)* Schools Council Research Studies, Macmillan Education

BULL, Ray and STEVENS, Julia (1976) 'Do we get 'A' for attractiveness?'; *Sesame*, December issue Open University

CARRÉ, Clive and HEAD, John (eds) (1974) *Through the Eyes of the Pupil* McGraw-Hill, for the Science Teacher Education Project

COX, Nancy (1976) 'Mrs Cox Eats Minced Morsels'; *English in Education* Vol 10 No 3. Aberdeen University Press, for NATE

CREBER, J.W. Patrick (1972) *Lost for Words* Penguin Education for NATE

CREBER, J.W. Patrick (1978) 'Theory meets Practice'; *Insight* Issue 1—3. Journal of the National Conference of Teachers' Centre Leaders

CURRIE, James (1884) *English Prose Composition* Blackwood

D'ARCY, Pat (1977) 'Writing Across the Curriculum — Changes in Attitudes?'; in Wilkinson & Hammond 1977

DAVIS, Frances and PARKER, Robert (eds) (1978) *Teaching for Literacy: Reflections on the Bullock Report* Ward Lock Educational

DES (1975) *A Language for Life* The Bullock Report HMSO

DIXON, John *et al* (1977) *Developing Active Comprehension* Schools Council Project English 16—19, Discussion Booklet No 3.

DOUGHTY, Peter (1968) *Current attitudes to written English, and their implications for the teacher of English* Longman, for the Schools Council Programme in Linguistics and English Teaching

DOUGHTY, Peter, PEARCE, John and THORNTON, Geoffrey (1972) *Exploring Language* Edward Arnold, for the Schools Council Programme in Linguistics and English Teaching

FRENCH, F.G. (1949) *Common Errors in English* Oxford University Press

GRAVES, Donald (1978) 'Bullock and beyond: research on the writing process'; in Davis and Parker 1978

H.M. INSPECTORATE (1977) *Curriculum 11—16* HMSO

HARRIS, Roland (1967) 'Some Thoughts on Research and the Teaching of English'; *English in Education* Vol 1 No 1. Bodley Head, for NATE

HARRISON, Colin and GARDNER, Keith (1977) 'The place of reading'; in Marland *et al* 1977

HARTOG, Sir Philip *et al* (1935) *An Examination of Examinations* Macmillan

McLUHAN, Marshall (1967) *The Medium is the Massage* Penguin

MARLAND, Michael *et al* (1977) *Language Across the Curriculum* Heinemann Educational

MARTIN, Nancy (1968) *Here, Now and Beyond* Oxford University Press

MARTIN, Nancy (1977a) 'Writing'; in Marland *et al* 1977

MARTIN, Nancy (1977b) 'Initiating'; in Marland *et al* 1977

MARTIN, Nancy *et al* (1976) *Writing and Learning Across the Curriculum 11–16* Ward Lock Educational

MEDWAY, Peter (1973) *From Talking to Writing* Originally published by the London Institute of Education. Reissued by Ward Lock Educational, for the Schools Council Project Writing Across the Curriculum 11–16, 1976

MULLER, Herbert J. (1967) *The Uses of English* Holt, Rinehart and Winston

NEWBOLT Report (1921) *The Teaching of English in England* HMSO

NORWOOD Report (1943) *Curriculum and Examinations in Secondary Schools* HMSO

ROSEN, Connie and Harold (1973) *The Language of Primary School Children* Penguin Education

SCHOOLS COUNCIL Working Paper No 3 (1965) *English: a programme for research and development in English teaching* HMSO

Working Paper No 9 (1967) *Standards in CSE and GCE: English and Maths* HMSO

Working Paper No 59 (1977) *Talking, writing and learning 8–13* Evans/Methuen Educational

TORBE, Mike (1976) *Language across the Curriculum: Guidelines for schools* Ward Lock Educational, for NATE

TORBE, Mike (1977) *Teaching Spelling* Ward Lock Educational

TORBE, Mike (1978) 'The secret-sharers: teachers' response to language across the curriculum'; in Davis and Parker 1978

TOUGH, Joan (1976) *Listening to Children Talking* Ward Lock Educational

WILLIAMS, Jeanette (1977) *Learning to Write, or Writing to Learn?* NFER

WILKINSON, Andrew (1975) *Language and Education* Oxford University Press

WILKINSON, Andrew and HAMMOND, Graham (eds) (1977) *Language for Learning* Exeter University School of Education

YOUNGMAN, M.B. and LUNZER, E.A. (1977) *Adjustment to Secondary Schooling* Nottingham University School of Education

ZUSSMAN, Barbara (1975) 'Just a tick is hopeless' Originally published by the Writing Across the Curriculum Project; quoted extensively in Nancy Martin *et al* 1976; and since reprinted in full in *Language Policies in Schools: Some Aspects and Approaches* Ward Lock Educational, for the Schools Council 1977